CHARGED WITH THE SPIRIT

CHARGED WITH THE SPIRIT

Mission Is for Everyone

Joseph G. Donders

ORBIS BOOKS

Maryknoll, New York 10545

The Catholic Foreign Mission Society of America (Maryknoll) recruits and trains people for overseas missionary service. Through Orbis Books, Maryknoll aims to foster the international dialogue that is essential to mission. The books published, however, reflect the opinions of their authors and are not the official position of the society.

Library of Congress Cataloging-in-Publication Data

Donders, Joseph G.
    Charged with the Spirit : mission is for everyone / Joseph G. Donders.
        p.   cm.
    Includes bibliographical references.
    ISBN 0-88344-915-3 (pbk.)
    1. Catholic Church—Missions.   2. Mission of the church.
3. Spiritual life—Catholic Church.   I. Title.
BV2180.D66   1993
266'.2—dc20   93-1613
                                                            CIP

*From the fullness of his grace we have all
received one blessing after another.*
(John the Baptist)

*You will receive power when the Holy Spirit
comes on you, and you will be my witnesses
. . . to the ends of the earth.*
(Jesus of Nazareth)

*A student is not above his teacher; but every
student when he has finished his studies will be
on a par with his teacher.*
(Jesus of Nazareth)

*For we cannot help speaking about what we
have seen and heard.*
(Simon Peter)

Contents

Introduction: Kindling the Divine Fire in Us   1

Part I
Catching the Depth of Jesus' Spirit

1. Meeting Jesus of Nazareth   7

2. Aroused by Jesus   13

3. Catching the Depth of Mary's Spirit   21

4. Beginning with Abram and Sarai   27

5. Prophetic and Messianic Imagery   34

6. Mary and Her Circle   40

7. Jesus' Self-Image   45

8. Gatherer of the Nations   50

9. Empowering and Liberating Healer   57

10. Reconciling Peace-Maker   64

11. Signs, Symbols, and Reality   72

12. Initiation, Spirit, and Mission   82

Part II
Fanning the Flame

13. Our Mission: Challenges and Priorities   91

14. How to Proclaim and Dialogue   99

15. The Why and How of Justice, Peace, and Creational Integrity   112

16. About Feeling at Home: Inculturation   123

17. How to Organize and Manage Our Mission   135

18. Victory and Celebration   146

Notes   153

CHARGED WITH THE SPIRIT

INTRODUCTION

Kindling the Divine Fire in Us

The Acts of the Apostles is the book about the failures and successes of the first communities formed by people who had met Jesus. A meeting that changed their lives. It tells how those communities sent people throughout their whole world. They also grew locally by attracting the people who lived around them. Luke speaks about that attraction when he—slightly ambiguously—notes:

No one else dared join them, though they were highly regarded by the people. Nevertheless, more and more men and women believed in the Lord and were added to their number (Acts 5:13-14).

The people they sent out did not do any lengthy preaching. Those first missionaries arrived, announced the good news, and shared the Spirit of Jesus (Acts 16:7). As a local community formed itself, the members began to live their newly shared Spirit and immediately began to tackle the religious, domestic, and social issues around them in a new way. They began to worship together, they shared the body and blood of Jesus, but they also started forms of what we would call social care. One community helped another community in economic need. Local communities started a soup kitchen in Jerusalem and a kind of thrift shop in Lydda, near Joppe. The communities had such influence

that in some cities they became a danger to the existing
official and corrupt order.

Why don't our communities send out people in that way?
Why aren't our own communities more attractive? Why is
our mission activity lacking in spirit? What has happened to
us?

Traditional mission activity and heritage has not waned
for lack of studies or analyses. Books about mission
abound, and an ever-growing number of audio and video
tapes accompany them. Not long ago a religious sociologist
gave a paper to a theological faculty in Washington, D.C.
He claimed that by the year 2020 the Catholic community
will be the largest denominational group in the United
States, comprising more than 50 percent of the population.
The tragedy, he said, is that this will make no difference to
the country. It is difficult to judge whether he is right or not,
but why does he think so? Is it true that the Roman Catholic
Church—and the other Christian churches as well—is an
irrelevant presence in a country like the United States? Do
we Catholic Americans, in other words, make no difference
to the world in which we live? Have our symbols lost their
impact on our own lives? Do we fail to offer an alternative to
a torn world that definitely—and desperately—is looking for
one? Have we no mission? Are there any signs left of the
appeal and fascination those first Christian communities
had for so many?

Many of us have experienced entering a church for a
Sunday service and noting that everything in the parish
seems to be dead. There are people, but they all seem gray,
even when dressed in bright colors. The singing seems
muted—booklets are opened, so are some mouths, but no
hymn is raised, no rhythm caught. The organ overpowers
the few small voices. The minister does all he is supposed
to do. The homily is well prepared. The collection baskets
go around. The service is liturgically correct. The members
of the congregation stand, kneel, sit down; they cross them-

selves. The service begins, continues, and ends without a whimper. Symbols are used, the word is spoken, bread broken, but the liturgy falls flat. The young are obviously bored; the older participants yawn behind their hands. After the service everyone moves out, some hands are shaken. The homily—some say—was interesting. Then they are on their way, the door of the church is firmly closed, and after a last look back, it is all over for the week. You decide never to come back if you can help it. You want to find another community. A caricature? Maybe . . .

And then you come into a community where everything breathes joy, hope, and spirit. You notice it when you come in; people welcome you with a smile here and a word there. The singing is taken up by all. The young sit with the old. Young people blow their trumpets and swing their tambourines, while the older solemnly beat their drums. Psalms are sung, and the hymns started by the choir are taken up by all: "Lord, have mercy, Christ have mercy. We share in the Glory of our Lord Jesus Christ, Alleluia!" The organ does not dominate, but is a help. It becomes silent, though perhaps a baby keeps bouncing its first vowels off the vault of the church. The story about God's people and Jesus is read with spirit, and the word is broken open for all in the homily. During the prayers of the faithful the intentions mention healing and sharing, peace and justice, environment and work, far-off lands and members sent out to have a taste of mission and community, perhaps on another continent. Then all turn their attention to the table and commemorate the presence of Jesus in the bread and the wine. People reach for one another's hands as they say the prayer that is going to change the whole of our still so cruel world: "Our Father in heaven . . . . your kingdom come, your will be done . . ." They share a sign of peace; the harm done and the distances created throughout the last week are overcome just before the bread and the wine go around. Every Sunday there are newcomers, and there is a regular list of people who would like to be baptized and confirmed. Those candidates stand near the baptismal font until the day they will publicly and formally share in the Spirit of Jesus present in the community and all its members. Once the service is over, the members divide spontaneously into small groups to discuss issues and tackle problems, which may or may not be solved. Their ministry to each other and the larger community is obvious and clearly collaborative. Tasks are given and received. Appointments are made while children play with each other outside, waiting for their parents to go home. There is laughter and good cheer. Simplicity and utter seriousness seem to go hand in hand. It is a joy to have been there. You decide to join them again when possible. You leave a better and divinely inspired human-divine being. You know again what you are about, living your life and doing your work.

Both types of parishes do exist. We all know about them. It is not difficult to guess the difference. It is not the Spirit of Jesus as such. That Spirit is present in both. It is in the sharing of that Spirit that they differ.

This book is about that sharing. How do we share Jesus' Spirit so that we personally and in our communities become sacraments of Jesus' presence in this world? How do we get coworkers in his mission to realize God's dreams for this world and our common future? To do so, we will have to go far back to the first time that a human couple began to see that future. (Was it from within or was it from without themselves?) We must share in that human/divine vision from its beginning to its fulfillment, sharing in a dynamic that is divine!

Let us, however, not get lost in that enormous upswing. This book also aims to be as practical as possible. It is not only written for personal reading, but also as a workbook for groups of Christians who come together to reconsider their place in the world and its history. Every chapter is followed by suggestions and questions to stimulate individuals and groups to reflect, to discuss, and to react.

Part I

CATCHING THE DEPTH OF JESUS' SPIRIT

CHAPTER 1

Meeting Jesus of Nazareth

Jesus himself drew near and went with them.
(Luke 24:15)

 chance encounter. It happens all the time. You talk to someone, and that stranger changes your life. It happens in planes, buses, waiting rooms, train stations, airport gates.

It happened about two thousand years ago for an Ethiopian minister of finance traveling home by horse-chariot (Acts 8:26). In Jerusalem he got something to read for his long voyage home. Being on a pilgrimage, he chose a sacred text—the Prophecies of Isaiah. The text was more difficult than he expected. It proved to be so difficult that he was reading it aloud, trying to catch the meaning of a particularly hard line:

He was led like a sheep to the slaughter, and as a lamb before the shearers is silent, so he did not open his mouth.

A young man heard what he was reading and asked: "Do you understand what you are reading?" He answered: "How can I unless someone helps me?" He invited the young man, this chance-met stranger who introduced himself as

Philip, to come in and sit next to him. It was during the discussion that followed that the government official heard the
good news of Jesus. The conversation must have been a
decisive one, because when they found some water alongside the road later in the day, they stopped and Philip baptized him. Philip engaged the African traveler—right there
alongside the road—in the dynamics of the risen life of
Jesus. We don't know much more about the official. Maybe
he was one of the founders of the still flourishing Ethiopian
Christian community. A chance encounter.

One day on a long flight the place next to me was empty.
A young fellow came from his empty row to the seat next to
mine. He asked me whether he could join me. We talked.
He told me about himself. We compared notes and noted
sympathies for points of view. We spoke about Jesus' place
in human life, and what we thought history would lead to.
We talked about what lies beyond this world, and what we
expected it all would lead to. An unexpected conversation.
Things I had never thought of fell in place. He spoke about
his expectations, and I about mine. A new horizon opened
up before me. The flight was over before I realized it. The
voice of the plane's captain surprised me when he
announced that we were descending to our destination, asking us to fasten our seat belts. I left the plane another person. A chance encounter.

The memory of such meetings doesn't wane. The experience is at times so enlightening that the enthusiasm created
does not fade. Human history is full of stories about such
meetings. No wonder that the Bible sometimes compares
these strangers with angels! A chance encounter—and life
changes forever.

THE ENCOUNTER WITH JESUS

This is how it was for those who encountered Jesus. People met him in the street, along the lake shore, at a well,

during the night, on a boat, on the road from Jerusalem to Emmaus, in the Temple, at their work. They met, and they started to talk. We are inclined to forget that the good news began in such a common way. Women and men, poor and rich, young and old walked up to him; they sat down, dined, wined, and ferried over the lake with him. They talked about their worries, their difficulties and disillusionment, about political rulers and accidents in the city. He in his turn told them his dreams and his hopes. He made them share in his dedication to the love of God. The world of those who listened to him changed. He kindled a fire in their hearts. They found meaning and new hope in their lives.

A chance encounter. No force, no threats, just an occasional meeting, a friendly contact, an open invitation. But the experience changed people completely. Men and women left everything behind to hear more, to be close, to follow him. He gave them self-respect, making them discover themselves, their deepest thoughts, their most daring dreams, the extent of their love. He reminded them of the old promises made by Yahweh to their ancestors. Things hidden were spoken aloud. Old and new dreams turned into reality. They discovered Yahweh—who seemed so far away in their worship and life—in their own hearts and in the hearts and minds of the companions around him. They remembered having heard before that something was happening in human history. They recalled events that had to do with their origin and destiny. They became aware again—though often only vaguely—that they as a people and as persons were taken up in a process. They recognized this process in the Sacred Scriptures read to them: the dreams of their prophets, the expectations of their visionaries, justice and peace, a period of grace to come. Things that too often had remained hidden in mystery and riddle. Here was Jesus, a simple carpenter they easily could relate to, a person of flesh and blood. He was like an artist who provokes sentiments and insights, inspirations and intuitions viewers never, or only vaguely, have been aware of. He made sense not only of the individual, but of the whole of life, marriage, work, children, failures and successes. He connected the person with the past, and opened him or her up to a future hardly dreamed about, even in youth.

The people listened, and they saw. He triggered something in them. He helped them tap into a reality hidden deep in them: the presence of God. The Second Vatican Council *Decree on the Church's Missionary Activity* describes this role of Jesus in our lives pointedly:

> This universal design of God for the salvation of the human race is not carried out exclusively in the soul of a man, with a kind of secrecy. Nor is it merely achieved through those multiple endeavors, including religious ones, by which men search for God, groping for Him that they may by chance find him, (though He is not far from any one of us) (cf. Acts 17:27). . . .
> . . .God determined to intervene in human history in a way both new and definitive. For He sent His Son, clothed in our flesh, in order that through this Son He might snatch men from the power of darkness and of Satan (cf. Col 1:13; Acts 10:38) and that in this Son He might reconcile the world to Himself (cf. 2 Cor 5:19).[1]

JESUS' ONGOING STORY

Those who encountered Jesus never forgot. If those meetings with him had not been so memorable his story would have ended. He would have been forgotten. But he is not forgotten. He remains the fascinating person he was to his mother, to men and women, to children in the street, to the academicians and politicians of his time. He showed by word and deed and work how we human beings are taken up in a process that is our common human mission, entrusted to us by God, our common source of existence. His memory has been manipulated at times to the point that many have been alienated from him. Yet people all over the world continue to tell his story and relate their discovery. He did not appear in this world to get lost and forgotten. He remains to millions a faithful companion, a person who roots them in the process of life itself. They cannot keep their story and its richness to themselves if they want to be faithful to that process. They understand that the wisdom of Jesus, the process of life, embraces the whole of humanity and the whole of creation. It is a vision that contains all. That is the reason that those who met him believed him to be divine. This book is about the consequences of that discovery for those who made it long ago, but especially for those of us who are meeting him now in the world in which we live. We will begin by considering the dynamics of such a meeting in the following chapter.

For Reflection

1. Can you recall a coincidental meeting that proved to be influential in your life? What happened to you at that time?

2. Did a chance encounter ever have a spiritual impact on you?

3. Have you ever changed the life of another through a chance encounter? Were you surprised to find that you had?

4. How have you met Jesus in your life?

5. Reread the above quotation from the Second Vatican Council's *Decree on the Church's Missionary Activity*. How does it relate to the kind of chance encounter this

chapter discusses? Can you give examples—physical, psychological, artistic, or spiritual—of potentialities that would have remained undiscovered in you except for a chance encounter with someone?

CHAPTER 2

Aroused by Jesus

*A student is not above his teacher; but every
student when he has finished his studies will be
on a par with his teacher.*

(Matthew 10:24-25)

W hat happens to us when we meet someone—a
teacher, a friend, a guru, a stranger, or someone
like Jesus—who moves us so much we are
changed? A simple question. A question we
should try to answer before we go on speaking about the
process that might be the result of such a meeting. Yet we
often don't stop to answer simple questions. We think we
know the answer, but we don't. Let me try to answer this
one by something that happened to me not so long ago.

A LESSON IN THE STREET

It was New Year's day in Melbourne. I walked home from
the post office, where I had been mailing late Christmas
mail. I heard sirens in the distance. It was difficult to tell
whether it was the police, an ambulance, or the fire brigade—or even where the noise was coming from. When I
turned the corner, I saw big clouds of smoke billowing out

13

of the windows and the front door of a house. Weeping women were standing in front of the house with children clutching their skirts. Men were shouting nervously to one another. One man put a wet towel over his face and tried to enter the house, but the smoke drove him back into the street.

Along with many others, I stopped to watch the scene. We all looked anxiously at the end of the street as the noise of the sirens became louder and louder. Finally the fire brigade arrived. In no time the firemen had jumped from their vehicle and connected hoses to the fire hydrant. Others unrolled hoses from their truck. They hosed the house down from the front to the back and from the back to the front, quickly bringing the fire under control; it did not even break through the roof.

When the greatest danger was over, the fire brigade commander took a notebook from his pocket and went to the family outside. He asked them the usual questions: "When did it start? Where did it start? Any idea how it started?" (At that question I saw a small boy suddenly hide behind his mother.) "Are you insured? With what company?"

Suddenly a woman who had been standing next to me burst into tears. I asked, "Do you know that family?"

She said: "No!"

"Do you know what happened?" I asked her.

Again she answered, "No!" Then she added, "What does it matter whether I know them or not? Just put yourself for a moment in their position—such a disaster on New Year's day!" Then, still crying, she went over to comfort the distressed family.

Suddenly I understood something that had puzzled and worried me for a long time. For years I had been involved in justice and peace work. For some time I was the Executive Director of the African Faith and Justice Network in Washington, D.C. The main task of our office was to inform its constituency, mainly religious congregations that had missionaries in Africa, about the situation there, and to stimulate them to pick up their phones or pens and to lobby the House of Representatives, the Senate, the president, or church leaders. We collected information from sources on the spot about famines, wars, infringements of human rights in that large continent. We sent that information out in the hope that our members would take action. Often they didn't. We thought perhaps the material we sent out was too long, so we made it shorter. Nothing changed. We made it clearer, longer, more in depth. Nothing helped.

I had been worrying and wondering about that lack of response. The fire in Melbourne was an eye-opener to me. The fire brigade was necessary; it was efficient; it did its job. The commander gathered all the data; when he closed his notebook and put his pencil away, he had an idea what had happened. But the woman next to me had reacted in another way. She sympathized, or better, empathized with the victims. She allowed her heart and mind to vibrate with their hearts and their minds. That is why she wept. That is why she walked over to ask them to come for a cup of coffee in her home.

RESONATING WITH JESUS' SONG

It is that kind of compassion—which means cosuffering—that makes persons take action. Our office on Africa had not been able to evoke that response in its members. Oh, it accumulated all the information, all the data, all the items that the fire brigade commander noted in his booklet. But it did not do what that woman next to me did, and asked me to do: "Just put yourself for a moment in their position." Join for a moment their lament. Sing their sad ballad. Jesus once complained: "I sang a sad song for you and you did not cry!" (Mt 11:17; Lk 7:32). He asks us to *feel* with him.

Paul of Tarsus did this. In one of his many letters he wrote to his friends in the Greek town Philippi: "I long for all of you *with the affection of Jesus*" (Phil 1:8). That is how translators translate the text. They do so to avoid the embarrassment a literal translation of the words would cause. What Paul really writes is that he longs for them with the "guts" of Jesus. Paul had Jesus' gut-level feelings. He reacts in Jesus' way. He wrote to another group of his friends, this time in Galatia: "I no longer live, but Christ lives in me" (Gal 2:20).

Jesus made something happen to Paul, just as he had done to his disciples before, and just as he would do to so many others afterward. He did it to me, and as you are interested in reading this book about him and his dynamics, he must have triggered something in you too. Not many of his disciples would repeat Paul's words about having Jesus' own gut-level feelings, but they do speak about having his spirit, "the Spirit of Jesus" (Acts 17:6), or in more recent times, about having the heart of Jesus. It comes to the same. They are "struck" by Jesus. They reverberate with him. They are on the same wavelength.

An example from the world of music might help to illustrate this point. A grand piano is standing in a spacious and open room. It is well tuned. The lid is open, and the snares and strings of the instrument are visible. You stand some distance from the piano with a tuning fork. You hit the tuning fork on the wood of a table and put it down on its stem. The vibration of the tone fills the whole room. You put your hand on the tuning fork to silence it. And—if all goes well!—the snare on the grand piano that corresponds to the tone of your tuning fork has picked up its vibration and is singing on its own. Something like that happened to Paul. There is something in him that made him react to Jesus. Jesus touched something in him. And he began to resonate with Jesus' own song.

The pain and sadness of the people around that burning

house in Melbourne triggered something in the heart and head of the woman next to me, her compassion. It is from within ourselves that we feel and react, even when stimulated by someone else. Jesus worked on that principle. He teaches us to drink from our own wells. He uses parables and stories to strike values and attitudes in his hearers. Once struck, once brought to life, they vibrate on their own, so to speak.

PLUCKING THE LISTENER'S HEARTSTRINGS

When I was teaching at the University of Nairobi in Kenya and preaching as university chaplain in the university church, one of my African colleagues came to me, obviously embarrassed. After some introductory chitchat he said, "I want to tell you something." I asked him what it was. He said: "I like your teaching and your preaching and so do many others, and yet . . . you do it in an other way than we Kenyans are accustomed to." It was obviously an invitation for me to ask for the nature of the difference. So I did. He explained that an African educator would tell a story, a good story, but he would not—as I tended to do— give an explanation of the story. When he saw that I did not get his point, he gave me an example of what he meant.

One day he discovered that his oldest son, Mungai, had told him a lie. Late in the evening, just before he went to bed, he called his son and told him a story I knew, and you may recognize too.

Once upon a time, a small boy named Kamau was asked to herd some goats for his grandparents. The grass was far from his grandparents' home, so far that Kamau could neither hear the voices of the people at home nor smell the smoke of their fires. One day, when he felt very lonely, he thought, "I know how to get my people here," and he turned toward the village and shouted as loudly as he could: "Lion, lion, help, help!" Everyone in the village who heard him jumped up, took a spear or bow and arrows, and ran to help Kamau. When they found no lion, they went home, telling each other, "Kamau is a liar!"

Some days later Kamau again became lonely in that great African plain, and he thought, "It worked last time, so let me try again." He turned toward the village and shouted, "Lion, lion, help, help!" The people all jumped up, took their spears and bows and arrows and ran to help him. They ran for nothing, for there was no lion. Walking home, they again said to each other, "Kamau is a liar!"

A week later Kamau was in the field with his goats when an enormous lion appeared from behind a bush. Kamau shouted, "Lion, lion, help, help!" But in the village the people did not jump up. They said to each other, "He must think we are crazy; he is a liar!" When Kamau did not return home that evening, they went to look for him. But they only found his stick and one of his sandals.

My friend then said to his son, "Did you hear that story, Mungai? All right, go to bed and sleep well."

And that, my friend told me, is that. You don't explain such a story. If you explain it, you not only suggest that your listeners are stupid, but in a way you steal their conscience away from them and replace it with yours. The wonder of telling a story is that it calls up values in those who listen to you. It makes them recall something that is *in them*. It helps them find out something about themselves.

This is what Jesus must have done to many people around him. They listened to him, they saw him, they touched him, and something in them vibrated. They heard the melody he sang resound in their hearts. That is how they recognized him as someone special, and that is why so many accompanied him. It is the reason they "converted" to him and changed their lives. He—and his stories—awakened something in them. His dynamic became theirs.

There are immense depths in us. There are fantastic possibilities, realities that remain hidden if we are not stimulated by someone else. John once said of Jesus that he came to baptize us with Holy Spirit and fire (Mt 3:11). Jesus himself said,"I have come to bring fire on earth, and how I wish it were already kindled!" (Lk 12:49). What was lighted in those who let themselves be affected? What was the change in their orientation? What was the difference Jesus made? What did they hear in themselves when they listened to him? What does it mean to be taken up in the process he launched here in our world? When and how do we begin to live his energy and his love? To answer those questions, we have to know more about him. One place to start is with his mother.

For Reflection

1. Are there times that others react to you only in a technical and formal way? Are there situations in which that approach is the one you prefer?

2. Why did Jesus prefer to tell parables and stories?

3. Do you ever tell stories in the hope of "striking a chord" in others?

4. Think about a story that has deeply influenced your life. Do you have a favorite gospel story that resonates with something inside you?

5. Here is a story. Does it relate to anything in the chapter?

    A sailing ship had been at sea for months and months. She was now miles out from the coast of Brazil and had been there for weeks. There was no wind; the ship had hardly moved. Rations were gone, and they had finished their drinking water. In the morning the crew could scrape some dew from the sails, but that was all.

The situation was desperate. Then one morning the lookout sees another ship—bigger, better equipped, and making some progress. At the shouts of the lookout, the captain immediately starts signaling to the other ship, "Please, send us some water, we are dying with thirst." The other ship signaled, "Lower your buckets right where you are!" The distressed captain couldn't believe his eyes, and again he signaled, "Please, send us fresh water, we are dying!" He gets the same return message. Those messages go on for quite some time, until the captain—in utter despair—lowers buckets into the ocean. And he draws up sparkling fresh water!

The ship was off the coast of Brazil, where the gigantic Amazon River pushes fresh water into the Atlantic Ocean for miles and miles.[1]

CHAPTER 3

Catching the Depth
of Mary's Spirit

*I will pour my Spirit on all people. Your sons
and daughters will prophesy, your young people
will see visions, and your old folks dream
dreams.*

(Acts 2:17)

Years ago the University of Nairobi in Kenya sponsored a project to interview "wise" people. First, students in the Department of Philosophy and Religious Studies looked in their own communities for men and women considered wise. They did this by finding out whom people consulted when they were in personal or communal difficulties. Once that research was done, they began systematically to interview those men and women. They did not ask them questions, because questions are leading. Rather, they asked them to speak about life, sickness, death, community, the dead, offspring, solidarity, courage, and such issues.

I sometimes joined in these interviews. Though I depended in most cases on interpreters, doing this was an amazing experience—like opening living treasure houses. Most of the wise people put the themes they discussed in contexts that led back into the past for hundreds or thousands of years. That word *past* is not really accurate, because they spoke about those events and experiences as still affecting their present lives. Talking with them was calling up an experience that we in the West are only rarely aware of. It was the vital connection with their past that made them wise in regard to the present and the future.

In a theological course for future ministers in Washington, D.C., a course called "The Practice of Interreligious Dialogue," a group of students listened to a Jewish rabbi. In his lecture he touched on the Holocaust, the destruction of the Jewish people during the Second World War in Nazi Germany. One of the students became impatient. He said that he couldn't understand why Jews could not forget that horror. "It happened more than fifty years ago," he added. The guest lecturer did not seem upset by this interruption. He asked for a Bible, opened it, and read from the book of Exodus. He read of far-off days, when a new pharaoh, who did not know Joseph's story, came to power in the land of Egypt. This pharaoh put slave masters over the Jews, forcing them to build for him the cities of Pithom and Rameses (Ex 1:8-11). The rabbi then put the Bible down and said: "Did Jesus ever forget what happened to his people in Egypt? Do you Christians ever forget it?" He explained the difference between forgiving and forgetting. Only forgiveness can heal the past. We should forgive, but we should never forget what happened, if only to avoid having it happen again.

The last supper Jesus had with his disciples was a Passover meal. During that meal the youngest of the company— was it John?—had to ask the ritual question, "Why are we here tonight together? What does make this night a special night?" Jesus gave the answers to that question the night of his own Passover. He connected the two events, the Passover they were celebrating and the Passover he was engaged in. The whole past of his people echoed that night at his table, together with all the promises made in view of a new future. To sit at that table with Jesus is being in touch with the history and the hopes not only of his people, but with the fate of the whole of humanity, the outcome of the whole of creation. It was to be part of the process, of God's plan.

MARY'S STORY

If we could sit at table with Jesus' mother, Mary, we would also have that kind of experience. If we asked her why she had been willing to bring Jesus into this world, then the same past and future, the same dreams and hopes would open up to us.

We often think of Mary as a simple, young, and pious woman living in a small village, Nazareth. But she was not as simple and naive as all that. That becomes obvious in the story of her meeting with Elizabeth. You remember the story. When an angel came to ask Mary's consent to conceive from the Holy Spirit and to give birth to the one all generations had been waiting for, she did not tell Joseph, the man she was betrothed to. Joseph heard what had happened to his fiancee later from another heavenly messenger. The angel who came to Mary told her also that her relative Elizabeth was pregnant, and that she was already in her sixth month. Elizabeth also had conceived in a miraculous way. She was old, beyond child-bearing age, when an angel appeared to her husband Zechariah during his temple service to tell him that he and his wife would give birth to a son. They were to call him John. Zechariah had never been able to tell Elizabeth; he had been struck dumb. Elizabeth conceived, and she was already in her sixth month when Mary received the news. We don't know what Mary eventually told Joseph, nor do we know what Elizabeth told her husband. What we *do* know is what the two women said to each other when they met. It is at that moment that Mary's world opens to us in her song:

> "My soul glorifies the Lord
> and my spirit glorifies in God, my Savior
> for he has been mindful of the humble state of
>   his servant.
> From now on all generations will call me blessed,
> for the Mighty One has done great things for me
> —holy is his name.
> His mercy extends to those who fear him,
> from generation to generation.
> He has performed mighty deeds with his arm;
> he has scattered those
> who are proud in their inmost thoughts.
> He has brought down rulers from their thrones
> but has lifted up the humble.
> He has filled the hungry with good things
> but he has sent the rich empty away.
> He has helped his servant Israel,
> remembering to be merciful to Abraham
> and his descendants for ever" (Lk 1:46-55).

Mary shows in this song the world in which she lived. It is the reaction of someone keenly aware of what is going on around her—the political intrigues and the power plays. It is the hymn of someone who not only made a kind of social analysis of the world in which she lived, but who was also keen on the role she had to play. It is the response of a woman who reached back to the very beginning of the history of her people and of the whole of humankind. She based her trust and never-ending hope on God's loving promises to her ancestors. She mentioned Abraham and his family by name. The whole history of her people and of the world, and all the promises and hopes ever expressed by them echo in her song, a song that sounds like a battle hymn. No wonder that even in our own world women sing Mary's liberation hymn when they come together to protest injustice and demand change.

Devout Jewish men and women dreamed of being involved in the bringing forth of the Messiah. They considered barrenness a scourge because it precluded the possibility of making a direct genetic contribution to that hoped-for coming. Elizabeth refers to these expectations when she too speaks about "a fulfillment of the things that have been spoken" (Lk 1:45).

GOD'S PLAN

Mary and Elizabeth, and Joseph and Zechariah too, were conscious of being taken up in a process that reached from the beginning of the world's history to its fulfillment. They did not know all the details. But they walked in faith. They walked faithfully according to the promises made to them. They were aware that something was going to happen, and they were willing to involve themselves in the dynamics of God's plans for this world. According to Mary's own words, that divine project had something to do with a promise of long ago, a promise made to Abraham, a promise that had made him and his wife Sarah "strangers in a strange land."

The things Abraham and Sarah only saw and welcomed from a distance (Heb 11:13) still had the power to make them move. Mary's and Elizabeth's awareness of being taken up in a process came from that earlier promise. So, if we want to understand better what made Mary agree so enthusiastically to become involved, we have to know what happened to Abram and his family.

For Reflection

1. Do you consider yourself to be taken up—*as a Christian*—in the dynamic process of the world's history?

2. Mary played a critical role in God's plan. How would you have reacted to what happened to Mary? Do you see yourself as invited to take part in her role in this world?

3. What promises help you to continue your journey?

4. Do you "echo with the past" in your view of the future?

5. Reread Mary's song. Does it strike you as having implications other than the religious and pious ones we usually associate with it—and with Mary?

6. How does Mary's story resonate with your own?

CHAPTER 4

Beginning with Abram and Sarai

For he was looking forward to the city with foundations, whose architect and builder is God.
(Hebrews 11:10)

A bram and his wife Sarai are the first traceable people mentioned in the Bible. By traceable we mean that we have material evidence of their existence; we can find their footprints; they left things behind we can lay our hands on. This is not to say that the persons who are mentioned in the Bible before them did not exist. They did, but we can't trace them. They have disappeared into a kind of mythical mist. We don't know where paradise was. And despite the efforts of many explorers, the ark of Noah remains hidden.

Abram and Sarai are different. We know they lived about four thousand years ago, and we know where. Abram lived in two cities, Ur and Haran, both situated in the land of the Chaldees and both excavated in recent years. Ur and Haran were similar in their worship; they worshiped a moon god named Sin. Excavation of their temples revealed that they sacrificed children to their moon god, probably their first-born in order to assure further fertility. Abram and Sarai—as they are called in the beginning of their story—decided to leave that environment. The Bible tells us that Yahweh asked them to do so (Gn 12:1-3). They could not agree with what was going on in Ur, so they moved to Haran, but finding the same difficulties, they left that city, too.

How they heard Yahweh's command to leave we don't know. Whether they heard it from God's presence in their own hearts or from a divine appearance we can only guess, but they did leave. That departure can't have been easy for them. Others must have thought they had lost their faith. They became nomads in the desert; Abram, Sarai, and their extended family had many adventures.

TO WALK WITH GOD

The point is that they walked their way and faithfully fulfilled their mission. The Bible often gives them as examples of how to walk with God. Mary followed the example of their faithfulness when she responded to the angel. Yet that is not the reason that Mary thinks of them when she sings her song in the company of Elizabeth. At that moment something else in the life of Abram and Sarai is in her mind—the promise made to them at the moment that Yahweh changes their names from Abram and Sarai to Abraham and Sarah (Gn 17:1-8). Yahweh promises them that Abraham will be "the father of the nations." The Judaic Holy Scriptures never mention Abraham without a reference to all nations. That is the promise Mary has in mind.

Take the night that Yahweh called them out of their tent in the desert and asked them to look into the sky at the stars. Abram, and most probably Sarai too, must have been amazed that they were asked to do so. They had left Ur and Haran because they felt that they should not stare at the moon and the stars any more (Jdt 5:3-9). Now Yahweh asked them to do so, and they did. Looking in the bright star-studded sky they saw for the first time something in between those stars that became the leading vision all through Judaic and Christian literature. As the letter to the Hebrews so much later will recount, they didn't see it clearly yet. They only had an inkling. They saw "from a distance" (Heb 11:13) and from afar "the city, with foundations, whose architect and builder is God" (Heb 11:10). This image is fully worked out in the last book of the Bible, the book of Revelation. John describes the end, when there will be one city. God will dwell in that city, and Jesus Christ, the Lamb, will be enthroned in it. All nations will come together to the city, each one bringing its own glory and honor (Rv 21:24-27). It is the final outcome of God's love project for the human family. It is our destiny, and our mission.

Abraham and Sarah did not see all that. They were just beginners. But they started to move in the direction of the promise, leaving Ur and then Haran, and journeying on. They endured all kinds of complications: the initial barrenness of Sarah; Abram's relation to his second wife, Hagar; Sarah's envy at the birth of Hagar's son Ishmael; and too many other adventures to mention. It was the beginning of a divinely inspired initiative, a new process that ultimately will lead to the gathering of the nations and the final peace, justice, and fulfillment the whole of humanity always has hoped for. This is a hope based on a contract: "I am God Almighty; walk before me and be blameless. I will confirm my covenant between me and you" (Gn 17:1-2). God signed this new pact by sending a torch of fire to scorch the sacrifices Abram and his family had put down on the earth as their part of the new human/divine covenant.

This covenant was not the first between God and the human family. Earlier the rainbow was given as a sign of God's covenant with Noah and his family. It would not be the last covenant either. Later Moses would come down from the mountain with his stone tablets. The later covenants did not replace or cancel the earlier. They clarified one another. The overall picture became clearer and clearer until finally it was no longer a picture but the living reality of Jesus Christ, Immanuel, "God with us."

But we are running ahead. Let us get back to Abraham and Sarah. It was on the occasion of this new covenant that Yahweh changed Abram's and Sarai's names, as we mentioned before. God added a vowel to Abram. God added something to the original, as if to indicate that what happened to Abram and to his family should happen to every one and to every family, clan, and ethnic group in the world. That is, we have to leave our old set-up, and remaining faithful to ourselves, enter the march toward that future that will bring us all together, each one carrying his or her own gift.

FAITHFUL TO THE VISION

We have still a long way to walk before we will reach that city described in Revelation. The rest of Abraham's story—Abraham, who was also the first person to be called a Hebrew (Gn 14:13)—and the story of his offspring makes that very clear. That story is at times so violent that we wonder just how the vision was carried on to the time of Mary and Elizabeth. How is it that the book containing the vision of that ultimate human/divine city at the same time tells of so many terrible battles? How is it that the descendants of the visionary Abraham tell about the gruesome battles they fought against others, even claiming that they were ordered to do so by Yahweh?

Now go, and attack the Amalekites and totally destroy everything that belongs to them, put to death men and women, children and infants, cattle and sheep, camels and donkeys (1 Sm 15:3).

It is even more amazing that these kinds of texts were not censored away by later editors. They could report and keep them, however, because they always read them against the background of prophets like Isaiah, who remained faithful to the vision. The events always were contained in the context of the promise, that the time would come when Abraham and Sarah's vision would be realized.

The final editors of the Hebrew Bible expressed that same conviction in the way they edited the Bible's final edition, in the way it came to us. They did that during the Babylonian exile, a terrible time for the Jews, surrounded as they were by enemies who often laughed at their humiliation—a time so terrible that they did not even find the courage to sing their own songs. They did, however, edit their Bible. In the midst of an alien people they remained faithful to their vision. They did not put Abram's story, the beginning of their own people, as the first chapter in their collection of books. Rather, they began with some creation stories, each conveying in its own way how the whole of humanity is born from one and the same womb. What Abraham and Sarah had seen as the final outcome, they projected as the beginning.

They even used a third approach to save the overall vision that the peoples belong together and should not use violence against one another. It is not a persuasive approach—some would say it is just an evasion—but nevertheless it has its merit. Instead of blaming themselves for the disasters they wrought, they told how Yahweh waged their wars for them. Just think of the description of the conquest of Jericho. *They* did not do anything. They just marched around the town seven times, blasting their trumpets and chanting their war slogans. They did not throw a stone. They did not fire a shot. It was at the seventh turn around the town that the whole city and all its ramparts and walls fell apart and turned into dust. It was *Yahweh* who was the warrior, who could be the warrior because Yahweh was the creator of all human beings, a God who sends rain over the good and the bad. God had given them a vision that one day the whole of humanity and the whole of creation would be together, though the path was long and often violent and the difficulties almost insurmountable.

THE VISIONARY SONG OF THE PROPHETS

The prophetic voice remained sure in all those difficulties. Just listen to Isaiah, a prophet Mary and Jesus would later quote:

> It will happen in the final days,
> that the mountain of Yahweh's house
> will rise higher than the mountains
> and tower above the heights.
> Then all the nations will stream to it,
> many peoples will come to it and say:
> Come, let us go up to the mountain of Yahweh,
> to the house of the God of Jacob. . . .
> They will hammer their swords into plowshares
> and their spears into sickles.
> Nation will not lift sword against nation,
> no longer will they learn how to make war
> (Is 2:1-4).

The prophets remained firmly convinced of Abraham's vision and Yahweh's promise to him and his family. They were also conscious of the difficulties that had to be overcome to fulfill that vision. They wondered how the promise ever would be fulfilled in the world as they knew it and as it is described in the Bible from the murder of Abel by Cain to their own exile in Babylon. That is how they received the inspiration that someone—a Messiah sent by Yahweh— would come to this world, to make a new beginning. This is the one Mary was willing and eager to bring into this world.

For Reflection

1. Can you see your own life in the light of the promises made to Abram and Sarai? What does that mean to you?

2. Would it be fair to say that Christians have reduced the Abrahamic vision of reaching the city of God to something that is almost exclusively personal?

3. How is Abraham and Sarah's vision significant for our time and age?

4. How can their vision counteract the meaninglessness so many seem to experience in their lives?

5. Can you appreciate Mary's eagerness to be involved in the Abrahamic dynamics?

CHAPTER 5

Prophetic and Messianic Imagery

My eyes have seen the king, the Lord Almighty.
(Isaiah 6:5)

I t seems to me that we often overlook what really happened to people in the Bible, because we think they are different from us. Not different because they lived in another time and age or in another region of the world. From that point of view they *do* differ from us. What I mean is that we make super-human beings of them. We make Mary so holy and precious that she is out of our reach; we can hardly compare ourselves with her. When we hear Paul say that he does not live any-more but that Christ lives in him, we think of Paul as very privileged and special. We risk not applying what he says to ourselves.

THE VOICE OF INSPIRATION

In the last chapter we spoke of how the prophets, and especially Isaiah, were inspired to think that God would send someone to help humanity forward on its way to the realization of Abraham's vision. It might be that those prophets were inspired by a voice from heaven. That is quite possible. But there is also another possibility. The voice of inspiration may have come from within themselves. They believed passionately in the force of God's promise to their ancestors—just as Mary did years later. They were well aware of how difficult the road to the fulfillment of that vision was. They saw around them a human behavior that wasn't too promising, to say the least. They reported one disaster after another. Yet they maintained their belief in the promise from God. It was the combination of those two things, their belief in that final outcome and the difficulties they experienced, that convinced them that God was going to send someone to help.

It was not a difficult conclusion to reach. We often use the same kind of reasoning. Coming out of church one day, I met an older woman standing at the door. Practically all the parishioners had gone. The last ones said goodbye to one another and dispersed in different directions. The woman stood there alone. I asked whether I could help her, whether she had been left by someone, whether I could take her somewhere. She thanked me for my offer, but said her son had promised to come to bring her home. I need not bother about her. So I left. About half an hour later I came back to the church, and she was still standing there. Again I asked her whether I could help her. Again she refused. I pointed out that something might have happened to keep her son from coming. In that case, she told me with a wide smile, he will send someone else to pick me up. At that moment a car came around the corner to pick her up, as she had believed it would.

FAITH IN GOD'S PROMISE

A prophet like Isaiah was convinced that Yahweh would be faithful and lead God's people to the New Jerusalem, that city of the promise. God's love is reliable. Isaiah was also sure that something had to happen to make this possible, for he was convinced that it would be very difficult if not impossible for humanity to reach that aim as things were. How could the disastrous harm individuals and nations did—and do—to each other be stopped? Besides, even if it was possible to end that violence, how could people be reconciled after the terrible things they did—and we do—to each other? Would it ever be possible to bring together what was torn apart? Yet, there was the promise! As a consequence of his pondering on these issues Isaiah began to foresee and to foretell that one day Yahweh would send a savior, a redeemer, a liberator to rally the world and its population. That is how he and other prophets began to sing the song of a helper, a servant of Yahweh, a Messiah, who would come to the aid of his people, of all peoples in the world. A savior who would make the final breakthrough possible. Isaiah sang about that future event as if it had happened already:

> Every warrior's boot in battle
> and every garment rolled in blood
> will be destined for burning,
> will be fuel for the fire.
> For to us a child is born,
> to us a son is given,
> and the government will be on his shoulders.
> And he will be called Wonderful Counselor,
> Mighty God, Everlasting Father,
> Prince of Peace (Is 9:5-6).

THE SUFFERING SERVANT

Isaiah foresees that this new human beginning, the Messiah, will be called Immanuel ("God with us"). He knows intuitively that this new beginning must be untouched by the past and yet rooted in the past, virginal. Touching the great mythic stories he foretells that even by his birth the great one, the Messiah, will be distinguished from other human beings. In short, it becomes clear to Isaiah as he ponders all this that the Messiah will be born of a virgin (Is 7:14). He also draws another conclusion. The Messiah will suffer dreadfully. He could, of course, come with divine power to force Israel and the nations to march toward their goal. The promise, however, was that humanity itself would decide to move in that direction; in the end we would be able to say Yahweh and we arrived at our destination. The promise to Abraham excluded force. The journey would remain a human one, one freely willed. The Messiah would operate within the context of our human world. Isaiah fore-saw that he would be welcomed by many, but also that many others would turn against him, and that he would lose his life in the process. But he would not be forsaken by God and would rise from the dead.

> He was oppressed and afflicted,
> yet he did not open his mouth,
> he was led like a lamb to the slaughter,
> and as a sheep before her shearers is silent,
> so he did not open his mouth (Is 53:7).

It is not disrespectful to say that one didn't have to be a great prophet to prophesy the suffering and death of the Messiah. Anyone who came to help humanity break through its resistance in fulfilling God's plan would meet that fate. That is still true of the world in which we live today. Anyone who wants to bring humanity a step nearer to the ideal of one human family meets resistance. Too many people don't want that gathering of the whole of humanity in justice and peace as yet.

THE PROPHETIC LOGIC

Do we want to see in fulfillment that vision Abraham and Sarah first glimpsed so dimly? We might think that we are in favor of it, but that often is because we have never really been put to the test. So many among us are rejected or attacked when they put themselves on the line for justice and peace—from a coach who wants to make a team inter-racial, to someone like Reverend Martin Luther King, Jr., who wanted to assure the rights of the communities we often call minorities.

Of course the Messiah would get into difficulty! Isaiah foresaw that his appearance would be disfigured beyond that of any human being, and his form would be marred beyond any human likeness (Is 52:14), but he would see his offspring and the intention of Yahweh would prosper in his hands (Is 53:10). His confidence in Yahweh's faithfulness to the promise made to Abraham's family combined with his insight into the actual sinful state of humanity made him expect God to send a Messiah. The same logic made him know that the Messiah would suffer and even be killed. But the promise would be kept, the Messiah would rise from destruction and death, and humanity's journey would con-tinue into its last stage. Mary and Jesus were aware of this prophetic logic. They both quote Isaiah when they explain to themselves and to others their mission, as we will see in the next chapter.

For Reflection

1. Do you agree with Isaiah's prophetic logic that if the promise made by Yahweh to Abraham is valid in a world like ours, then a Messiah should come to us?

2. Can you remember a situation in your life when you had absolute confidence in a promise?

3. Why did Isaiah expect the Messiah to suffer? Discuss that expectation in relation to a contemporary martyr for the cause of justice and peace.

4. Have you ever acted for the cause of "gathering the nations" into God's friendly family by attempting to open your family, circle, club, community, or organization to "strangers"? What was the result?

CHAPTER 6

Mary and Her Circle

*Look! The virgin is with child and will give birth
to a son whom they will call Immanuel.*
                    (Matthew 1:23; Isaiah 7:14)

T he information about the person of Mary is
sparse. We have no idea what she looked like or
how old she was when the angel addressed her,
though we might have a good guess. We do
have information about her spiritual life, about what moved
her. For example, when the angel invited her to be the
mother of the savior, she did not ask her heavenly guest
what his message was about; she knew that. Later, she
showed that she understood what was at stake when she
sang her song upon meeting Elizabeth. Speaking about herself she quotes the prophet Isaiah: "My soul proclaims the
greatness of the Lord" (Is 61:10), and speaking about her
future son, she quotes Isaiah again, saying that her son is
"coming to the help of Israel" (Is 41:9). She must have
known that Isaiah foresaw that the Messiah would be born
of a virgin (Is 7:14). What she did not know was how this
would happen, how it would come about. So that was her
question to the angel. The angel answered her question:
she will conceive from the Holy Spirit. Once the angel had
clarified that, Mary had no further difficulty. On the contrary,

she sang—quoting Isaiah. She rejoiced in her call, not only because of herself, but because of her people and the whole of humanity. She had hoped and prayed for this event. She carried in herself all the expectations of her people. She was the best expression of humanity's longings. Using an image from our first chapter, she resonated with all the hopes of those who went before her.

REJOICING IN THE PROMISE

Yet, according to Luke, Mary was not the only one who thrived on those hopes and expectations. Once Zechariah, Elizabeth's husband, could speak again (after the birth of their son, John), Luke reports that he also sang a song describing not only what happened to him and his family, but also how he saw the role of his son. Like Mary in her song, he went all the way back to the promise Yahweh made to Abraham and his family. He alluded three times to Isaiah when relating his son, John, to the fulfillment of that promise and to the dynamics that further it. He sang that people would call John Prophet of the Most High, and that he would prepare a way for the Lord (Is 40:3), who will give light to those who live in darkness and the shadow of death (Is 42:7), and will guide their feet into the way of peace (Is 11:6).

There are others in Mary's circle who were aware of what was happening. They didn't see her and her child as just another mother and child. They tuned in to the energy that could be felt in her and in Jesus. They were aware of the dynamics that were at work. When Mary and Joseph went to the Temple to present their child, two other prophetic people came out of the Temple's shadow: Simeon and Anna. Simeon asked them to allow him to hold the child Jesus, and he said:

Now, Master, you are letting your servant go in
     peace
as you promised;
for my eyes have seen your salvation
which you have prepared in the sight of the
     nations,
a light for revelation to the gentiles
and for glory for your people Israel (Lk 2:29-32).

In this short blessing of himself he quotes Isaiah four
times! No one in Mary's circle expressed the reason for
Jesus' coming more clearly: *all the nations are going to be
blessed because of the one who is born here.* He is going
to assure salvation to all. He is going help the whole of
humanity on its way to the common goal. Because he sees
this so well, he is also the one who sees best what this is
going to mean for the baby he has in his arms and for his
mother: "Look, he is destined for the fall and the rise of
many in Israel, destined to be a sign that is opposed," and
looking at Mary he adds, "and a sword will pierce your heart
too" (Lk 2:34). Mary and Joseph did not need much proof
of that—very soon afterward they are on their way to Egypt,
fleeing from Herod's terror. Refugees in Africa! When they
come back, they are not allowed to return to Bethlehem as
they had hoped to do. They live as refugees in Nazareth, a
little settlement of no importance.

JOHN THE BAPTIZER

Among Mary's family there is another person alive to
what is happening: John the Baptizer. Out in the desert and
baptizing masses of people, priests and other officials come
to ask him to give account of what he is trying to do. They
ask him who he is. They try to place him in what they know
of Messianic dynamics. Is he the Christ? Is he Elijah? Who is
he? John replies, again quoting—in his turn—Isaiah:

A voice of one that cries in the desert:
prepare a way for the Lord.
Make *his* paths straight (Jn 1:23).

Using the words "make his paths straight," John connects what he is doing in the River Jordan to a journey. His
words recall what Abraham and Sarah first glimpsed when
looking at the stars in the sky—the new city of God and
humanity. John refers to a trek that will lead to the great
gathering at the end of these days. His words echo what
Isaiah prophesied, that in the last days all nations will
stream together, affirming Yahweh's promise to Abraham, a
gathering that assures the salvation of the whole of the
human family and of every individual person willing to walk
that way.

BROUGHT TOGETHER IN GOD

It is this path Mary wanted to walk. We too often think of
salvation as something personal. But that kind of salvation
was not Mary's only concern. Her personal destiny definitely
is included in her vision; she is very aware of her personal
role and vocation. But, as all the prophets do, she sees her
personal destiny linked to a salvation that is much larger in
scope, a salvation by which the whole of humanity, the peoples of all times and the whole of creation, will find the fullness of life. Personal conversion is a basic part of it. John
the Baptizer makes that clear when he asks the people to
convert and be baptized. But that is not all. John asks them
to do so within a wider context—that of the whole of
humanity:

Let every valley be filled in,
every mountain and hill be leveled,
winding ways be straightened

and rough paths made smooth,
and all humanity will see the salvation of God
          (Lk 3:5-6).

The whole of existence is connected and should be brought together in God. That is God's promise and the vision of Abraham and Sarah, Isaiah, John the Baptizer, Mary, Zechariah, Elizabeth, Simeon, and especially Mary's son, Jesus! Would that the human family saw it more clearly!

For Reflection

1. Does this prophetic vision of God's plan and promise play any role in your life?

2. Do you see Mary as one who shared the vision of the prophets? Discuss.

3. Do you see your personal life journey in the context of a movement of all humanity? Explain.

4. How has the common Christian understanding of salvation broadened in recent times beyond the personal? Are you expressing that new understanding in the practice of your life?

5. Do you relate Jesus' mission to your life? Discuss this issue in your community.

CHAPTER 7

Jesus' Self-Image

The Spirit of the Lord is on me, because he has anointed me to preach the good news to the poor.

(Luke 4:18; Isaiah 61:1)

The village of Nazareth was humming with rumors. Jesus, who had left some months before, was back in town for the weekend. The rumors whispered that he had joined some others who went to be baptized by John the Baptizer. Something had happened to him at that baptism that had happened to no one else—something about heaven breaking open, a dove coming down, and a voice being heard. He had disappeared after that, so nobody could ask him about it. It seemed that he was in the desert for forty days, alone, where the devil tempted him. He had come out of the desert, and instead of coming back to Nazareth, he had started to travel around in Galilee, preaching in synagogues. Rumor said that he had a house in Capernaum, where he had been preaching to crowds in the streets. There were rumors about miraculous healings and the driving away of evil spirits.

SABBATH IN NAZARETH

Now he is home. It is time for him to explain what happened to him, why he did not settle at home after discovering his powers. He should account for his behavior.

The people of Nazareth knew that they could expect him to come to the synagogue service. Luke notes that it was his custom to do so. That Sabbath day the whole of Nazareth must have been there. When the time came for someone to do the reading, they all remained sitting. Nobody volunteered. They did not look at him, but they were waiting for him. They expected him to do the reading. He obliged. Luke does not explain whether he asked for the scroll of Isaiah, or whether they gave it to him. Whatever was the case, he ended with the book of Isaiah in his hands. He rolled it down until he had found the text he wanted to read:

> The Spirit of the Lord is on me,
> because he has anointed me
> to preach good news to the poor.
> He has sent me to proclaim freedom for the
>   prisoners
> and recovery of sight for the blind,
> to release the oppressed,
> to proclaim the year of God's favor
>   (Lk 4:18-19; Is 61:1-2).

Those who knew the text well must have been surprised that he ended his reading like that, for he did not finish the second verse. He stopped in the middle of it. He mentioned the proclamation of the year of God's favor, but he did not quote the continuation of that verse: "to proclaim the year of God's favor, *and the day of vengeance of our God . . .*" Not finishing the sentence from Isaiah, he sat down, a sign that he was going to speak and to teach. The tension in the synagogue became almost unbearable. Luke writes: "The eyes of everyone in the synagogue were fastened on him." Jesus looked at them, and said: "Today this scripture is fulfilled in your hearing." They all were delighted. This was more than they had been hoping for. He had announced that he was the one who was going to do the things Isaiah had prophesied for the last days. He announced that he was going to begin the final year of grace — the year of the Jubilee, as they sometimes called it.

This was the time that all wrongs would be straightened out, all wounds would be healed, and Israel restored in its full glory. They were enthusiastic about "the gracious words" that came from his lips. They wondered how this could happen to Joseph's son, whom they knew so well, but they were quite willing to accept what he said. The rumors they had heard proved to be true after all.

A YEAR OF GRACE FOR ALL

Jesus then tackled directly the problem they had with him: "Surely you will quote this proverb to me: 'Physician, heal yourself! Do here in your hometown what we have heard that you did in Capernaum' "(Lk 4:2). He explained that this year of grace was not for them or for Israel alone. He gave the examples of a non-Jewish widow in Zeraphat and a Syrian army commander to illustrate that what he came to do would touch the whole of the world and all its population. At that moment the mood in the synagogue changed completely. If the year of grace was not for them alone, they did not want it. They could not bear the idea of having to share with aliens and pagans. If that was what he wanted, away with him. They became so angry that they jumped up, threw him out of their synagogue, pushed and pulled him out of town to the brow of the hill on which their town was built in order to throw him down the cliff. Jesus did what anyone should do in such a situation. Don't show an angry crowd your back, but face them. That is what he did. He turned around, faced them, and walked right through the crowd and went on his way (Lk 4:25-30).

It is easy to blame those villagers. But we should not do so before making sure that we ourselves are free from that kind of envy! We meet their refusal to share in the reluctance of so many to receive refugees and immigrants, to be with the poor and sick, to take care of the young and the old, to accept strangers and those who don't share our beliefs and customs. We hope for yet fear and resist God's promise of oneness.

Jesus went back to Capernaum. The people of Nazareth must have been wondering about Capernaum, a harbor and bordertown full of sailors, smugglers, minorities, and aliens from all over. It had a bad reputation. It was—though in a modest way—the most cosmopolitan town in the region Jesus covered. Galilee was the least Jewish region of Palestine, and Capernaum was the least Galilean town in the neighborhood. It was in the streets, on the squares, and in the synagogues of that town, a gathering point of all kinds of people and nations, that Jesus preached for the first time the coming of God's kingdom.

The incident in Nazareth shows that from the beginning of his preaching and healing Jesus saw his mission as universal, touching the whole of the world. He had come to help humanity on its way to the fulfillment of Abraham and Sarah's vision; he had come to honor the promises made to Abraham and Sarah and their family, and through them to all the nations of the earth. That is what he told them in Nazareth when he applied Isaiah's prophecies to himself, when he told them that he had not come only for them but for the whole world. Jesus lived those words in his deeds. He moved from Nazareth to Capernaum, a move from the province into the world. It is from Capernaum that he starts his mission, full of the divine dynamics of God's Spirit. He had come to gather the nations, to fulfill God's dream about humanity. This was the dynamic he wanted to share. He began to look around for company.

For Reflection

1. Discuss some contemporary situations that mirror Nazareth's refusal to share salvation. Is the reluctance to accept immigrants and refugees, mentioned in the chapter, a valid comparison?

2. Liberation theologians often take Jesus' reading of Isaiah at Nazareth as the starting point for their theology. Why would they do this?

3. Is it correct to say that Jesus "opts for the poor" in the incident in the synagogue at Nazareth?

4. Humanity's journey to the new city began with Abraham and Sarah, who moved from Ur and Haran because of their beliefs. Now we see Jesus acting on his beliefs by moving from Nazareth to Capernaum. A journey begins with movement. Do you know of anyone who moved from one place to another because of his or her convictions?

CHAPTER 8

Gatherer of the Nations

He who does not gather with me, scatters.
(Luke 11:23)

J esus' weekend appearance in Nazareth was a failure. It is interesting to look at the nature of that fiasco. It was a portent of what his difficulty would be. It was the first time that he faced a death threat, a threat uttered because he wanted to move the whole of humanity on its way to fulfillment. The people in the synagogue in Nazareth were eager to enter that fulfillment and period of grace for themselves, but they were unwilling to do so with others. They had difficulties opening their circle; they hesitated to live in a larger tent than they were accustomed to, to sit together with others at an expanded common table. They had been dreaming about Yahweh's promise to Abraham and Sarah and thus to them. They knew about Isaiah's prophecies, but they were not prepared to begin living that dream in the reality of their lives.

Every time Jesus opens the circle of the people around him, every time he breaks their restrictive taboos, he encounters resistance. It is not only in Nazareth that he gets death threats. The first time his life is threatened by priests in the gospel of Mark—considered by many as being the first gospel written—is during the so-called purification of the Temple. This is the story.

THE PURIFICATION OF THE TEMPLE

Jesus had been to the Temple the evening before. He had looked at everything, Mark notes, but since it was already late, he and his company had gone to Bethany for the night (Mk 11:11). The next morning they return to the Temple. Jesus interrupts the business done in the Temple. He throws over the bankers' stalls, and money rolls everywhere. He kicks over the stools of the sellers of sacrificial animals, and clouds of pigeons and doves fly up. He does more. He does not allow people to pass over the Temple square, which means that he essentially stopped the Temple service. The priests waiting in the back of the Temple for the next animal to be sacrificed wait in vain. Nobody turns up. They hear a man preaching at the entrance of the Temple: "Is it not written: 'My house will be called a house of prayer *for all nations!*' " (Mk 11:15). What he says echoes the promise to Abraham and Sarah. It is a realization of Isaiah's prophecy, the very mission of the Messiah in this world. It is then, Mark notes, that the priests and scribes came and "began looking for a way to kill him" (Mk 11:18). Mark doesn't mince words. He also mentions the reason they wanted to kill him: fear. They were afraid of the consequences of that gathering of all those nations.

We find the same fear among his own disciples. John tells a story about their hesitation. According to some biblical scholars the incident is the turning point in the gospel of John. Just before this story starts, John briefs us that the Pharisees told each other, "Look how *the whole world* is going after him!" (Jn 12:19). How right they were! This report follows that remark.

"MY HOUR HAS COME"

Some Greeks had come to the celebrations in Jerusalem. They approach Philip, the only one among the twelve with a

Greek-sounding name, and they tell him, "Sir, we would like to see Jesus" (Jn 12:21). It is obvious from the way John tells his story that Philip does not know what to do with this. He goes to Andrew, as he does often when he is in doubt, to ask his advice. We don't know what they discussed. Did they hesitate because they did not like to introduce Greeks at their common table? That would not be surprising; in those days the Greeks were a cultural threat to the Jewish traditions. The two, Philip and Andrew, decide to see Jesus about it. They tell him some Greeks would like to see him. Jesus' response must have been a surprise to them. Jesus says, "The hour has come for the Son of Man to be glorified." It is as if he is saying, "This is what I have been waiting for. Finally, things are starting to fall in place."

Earlier, at the wedding feast at Cana, Jesus said the hour "had not yet come." You remember the story. Jesus' mother was there together with the guests, family members, and their acquaintances—a very homogeneous group. Jesus and the disciples had been invited. It is difficult to know what went on in the heart and mind of Mary when she went to Jesus to tell him the wine was gone. Was Mary thinking of those passages in Sacred Scripture that describe the final outcome of our human journey toward God as a wedding feast—a wedding feast with plenty of food and plenty of wine? Did she get somewhat over-enthusiastic when she saw her son arrive at this wedding? Some exegetes, and many mystics, think so. There are good reasons for their opinion. Jesus himself often used the image of a wedding feast to describe the final outcome of the human pilgrimage toward God. Seeing her son at the wedding feast, Mary might have thought, "it might all start today, the hour has come, *his* hour has come!" She then went to Jesus to give him a hint of her guess. She tells him, "They have no wine," meaning they are waiting for the definite wine, the wine of the end, the wine of the kingdom, the wine of the New Jerusalem. Jesus answers, "Woman, what have I to do with you? My hour has not yet come!"

At Cana the hour had not come. When Philip and Andrew announce the arrival of the Greeks, Jesus says, "My hour has come." What is the difference between these two occasions? One difference is that at Cana only one sort of people were present, a homogeneous group of family members, friends, acquaintances, and neighbors closely related to one another. The gathering at Cana could not be seen as a fulfillment of either Abraham's vision or of Isaiah's prophecy of "all nations coming together." It was too restricted a group.

But when Philip and Andrew come to Jesus with their message that some Greeks want to see him, the situation is different. The Jewish contemporaries of Jesus' Greeks were not only strangers and outsiders. They were their diametrical opposites. The Romans were a military and political danger, a danger the Jews knew what to do about. The Greeks were a danger that rooted more deeply. They were a threat to Jewish civilization and culture. The ways Greeks dressed, ate, philosophized, socialized, and organized themselves were a constant temptation to the Jewish nation. Greeks were the most unlikely people to join a Jewish movement like the one growing around Jesus. No wonder Philip did not decide on his own what to do when he was approached by some of them! He goes to his friend Andrew, and together they go to Jesus with their message. They had seen that Jesus did not mind relating to strangers. They had seen him deal with a Roman officer, a Samaritan woman, a Syro-Phoenician woman, and all kinds of other people, but what about those Greeks? What would the end be of all this socializing? As the alarmed Pharisees had been telling each other, "The whole world has gone after him!"

REALIZATION OF THE VISION

For Jesus, this was the realization of Abraham's vision. His hour had really come. Humanity had begun to gather as

God's one family. Philip and Andrew don't seem to have reacted too eagerly to Jesus' response. They needed further explanation, so Jesus tells them:

> I tell you the truth, unless a kernel of wheat falls to the ground and dies, it remains only a single seed. But if it dies it produces many seeds (Jn 12:24).

In other words, if the circle does not open up, it will remain fruitless. Open your circle, expand your tent, add places to your table!

All through the gospels Jesus exemplifies this attitude. He talks in public to women he should not have talked to. He was interested in children neglected by almost everyone. He wasn't afraid when lepers and other people considered impure approached him. He sat down with sinners and strangers. He asked his disciples again and again to get to the other side of the lake, the side they don't want to go to because it is foreign country to them, full of strangers. He uses signs and symbols to explain the universality of his mission. Once he sends the twelve out on their mission, indicating that they should cover the twelve tribes of Israel.

Another time he commissions seventy-two of them, probably with a reference to the seventy-two grandsons of Noah, who one day were sent out from the homestead of their grandfather to be the beginning of all the nations on earth (Gn 10:32). The number seventy-two, then, indicates that Jesus' disciples are being sent out to the whole of humanity. He is preparing them for the moment that he will send them and all his followers to the ends of the earth!

Jesus describes himself as someone who came to bring the harvest together, as a fisherman who brings the fish together in his nets, as a hen who gathers her chickens under her wings. At his last breakfast with his disciples he lets Peter and his companions catch 153 sizable fish. According to Saint Jerome, that number 153 was the com-

plete list of different types of fish known in that region at
that time. If that is true, it is another indication that he was
to bring all of us together. He speaks about the final homecoming of the human family—Yahweh's promise to Abraham—as a great banquet. He loves to organize gigantic
picnics in the open where thousands of people come
together and are fed. He will die—as the high priest Caia-
phas unwittingly attests—"for the scattered children of God,
to bring them together and make them one" (Jn 11:52).

JESUS THE GATHERER

Mark tells a story in which Jesus' outreach to absolutely
every human being is perhaps best illustrated. It is the story
about a possessed man in the land of the Gerasenes. Mark
could not have put that man any further away from normal-
ity. He lived at the other, the pagan side of the lake. He
lived in a cemetery, an unclean place for a Jew. People
chained his hands and his feet, but he tore everything apart.
No one dared to approach him anymore. He behaved as a
wild man, shouting among the tombs at night and cutting
himself with stones. He lived with pigs nearby, for a Jew
another horror. He was possessed not by one, but by a
legion of evil spirits. Mark did everything possible to
describe the man and his world as alien. He even adds that
the people in the villages around did not take kindly to
Jesus. If there was ever a marginalized human being it was
this man in Gerasa. Everyone in the region was deadly
afraid of him; he was a non-person. Yet Jesus asks his disciples to bring him to that side of the lake, where the man
is raging around. When the man comes to him, he meets
him, chases the demons out of him, and heals him. In the
end of the story Jesus sends him home to his family to tell
them what the Lord had done for him.

Jesus' outreach as a gatherer is all-embracing. He does

not exclude anyone; he is divine in his approach. He displays the attitude of God, who lets his rain fall over the good ones and the evil ones. He tells his followers to love their enemies, that we belong together. We are invited not only to listen to what he says but to live as he lives, to be as he is. Those who refuse to follow his example, those who divide humanity, considering themselves as the only chosen ones, fear him. For their exclusive attitude Jesus had no good word. When he met them, he spoke in terms of vipers and whitewashed tombs, of hypocrites who falsely called themselves sons and daughters of Abraham. In his vision the whole of humanity was blessed and vivified by the same call and mission. Bringing us together would heal all of us. It is the reason he called himself a physician, a healer, as we will see in the next chapter.

For Reflection

1. In 1948 the Nobel Prize-winning astronomer Sir Fred Hoyle said: "Once a photograph of the earth, taken from the outside, is available . . . a new idea as powerful as any in history will be let loose." Discuss.

2. The photographs Hoyle asked for have since been taken. How do they compare with what Abraham and Sarah saw when they were asked by God to look at the stars?

3. Philosopher Karl Popper once wrote that the norm to test a society is its care for its weakest members. What do you think of that norm from Jesus' point of view?

4. We say that "God listens to the cries of the poor." Has this something to do with Jesus' outreach to the marginalized?

CHAPTER 9

Empowering and Liberating Healer

And he said to her, "Daughter, your faith has made you whole; go in peace."

(Luke 8:48)

L uke was most likely a medical doctor. There are many reasons for this traditional belief. One is that he has Jesus introduce himself as a doctor to the villagers in Nazareth. At another time in Luke's gospel Jesus says that he did not come for the healthy, but for the sick. He says this when he is blamed for eating and drinking with sinners. His healing reaches beyond physical and psychological sickness to spiritual defects, addictions, aberrations, and sinfulness. When he sends his disciples out, he gives them his healing power. He sends them out to announce the kingdom, to convert people, to chase evil spirits, and to heal the sick. The gospel is full of his healings. Sometimes he touches people; at other times people touch him. In most of the cases Jesus rounds off his healing by telling the healed ones, "Your faith has healed you." It is something in the sick persons that makes them whole again. This does not mean that he does not do anything to them. He does, but the healing he brings about also has something to do with the sick person in question, or sometimes with people related to them. It always has.

THE POWER OF FAITH

Healing comes from a power within. The doctor plays the role of a midwife, trying to help us give birth to the energy and the life power that will overcome our illness. Healing differs from chasing something away. You can chase away an evil spirit, but you can't chase away a physical sickness. It has to be healed from within. When that inner restorative power is not present there can be no healing. Jesus often calls that power faith. Mark tell us that once in his own region Jesus could not work any "mighty work" (Mk 6:5), because the people in question refused to tap that power in themselves. It is a power he finds in people written off by their fellow citizens and their religious leaders, in lepers and people born blind, deaf, and mute. He finds it in a Roman officer, a Samaritan woman, a Syro-Phoenician mother. He is a healer to them all, empowering them to stand up, walk, see, hear, speak, and react. He not only prompts physical healing in this way, but he helps victims to overcome their addictions.

ZACCHAEUS

Luke gives us a case study of this in the story of Zacchaeus, the money-addicted tax collector. Before he left his house he carefully locked his money box, the drawer in which he kept his money box, the door of his office, and finally the door of the building. He was rich, a chief tax collector, and small of stature. His smallness was not only of body. Between the lines of the story we can read that his self-esteem was not much bigger. Maybe he even hated

himself; people who are only after money often do. No wonder that the people in town considered him to be just plain
mean.

Zacchaeus knows that he will have no chance to see
Jesus, being so small and hated. Nobody is going to make
room for him in the front row. So he climbs up into a tree
to see Jesus. And Jesus looks up and calls Zacchaeus
down, saying, "Today I am going to stay in your house."
Zacchaeus came down as quickly as he could; he practically
fell out of the tree in his haste to receive Jesus well. At once
the people around begin to murmur, "He is staying with a
man who is no good." Jesus responds, "He is also a son of
Abraham!" By saying this he touches in the addict Zacchaeus his real worth, the old vision, which he has lost in
his life. Stimulating that vision, teasing it out, he makes
Zacchaeus alive to himself, so that he even reevaluates his
view of money, "Lord, half of my goods I give to the poor,
and if I have wrongfully exacted anything from anyone, I will
restore it fourfold." Zacchaeus is himself again and on his
way to Abraham's vision!

THE GOOD NEWS FROM WITHIN

Jesus often speaks about the fish that has to be caught,
the pearl that has to be found, the treasure that has to be
dug out, or producing things from a cupboard that holds all
kinds of things, old and new. He is constantly helping others to do that fishing, finding, digging, and producing from
within themselves. He is a passionate believer in the good
work God did when putting us together. The good news he
brings reminds us of our often forgotten common divine
origin. Notwithstanding all that has happened to the human
family and its world, God remains faithful. The divine breath
blown into all of us from the very beginning never has left
us. The divine spark might be smoldering almost invisibly

under piles of ashes, but the spark is still there. One of the
most touching descriptions of Jesus' renewing activity is
when Matthew applies to him this old prophecy of Isaiah:

> He will not shout or cry out, or raise his voice in the
> streets. A bruised reed he will not break, and a smol-
> dering wick he will not snuff out, till he leads justice to
> victory (Mt 12:20; Is 42:3).

THE ADULTEROUS WOMAN

Another occurrence, this one in the gospel of John, also
illustrates Jesus' approach well. It is the incident of the adulterous woman. Let us analyze what happens in this story. It
is early in the morning when Jesus comes to the Temple.
He does not enter it but sits down somewhere near by.
Some people surround him, and he begins teaching them,
telling stories and asking questions. At some point they hear
noise in the distance, a threatening noise, the noise of an
excited crowd. Then they see a group of men with stones
and sticks in their hands surrounding someone whom they
push and pull about. As the group gets nearer, the people
around Jesus can see what is going on. A riotous group of
men are manhandling a woman, who hardly manages to
keep herself upright. She obviously has had no time to get
properly dressed. Her husband had come home unexpect-
edly and caught her with another man, who escaped. She
was caught. Neighbors joined the commotion, elders and
some Pharisees were called in, and the mob decided to
stone her outside the city. Then one of the Pharisees got an
idea. Why not use this woman to trap Jesus? He proposed
to the others that they take her to Jesus to ask whether they
should stone her to death. Whatever answer Jesus would
give, he reckoned, could afterward be used against him. If
he said, "Yes, stone her!" that story could be told all over

the country. If he said, "No, don't stone her!" the story
would be that Jesus did not obey God's law given to Moses,
to stone such a woman.

The group arrives before Jesus, who hardly looks up.
They tell him what happened and ask him what he suggests
they do. Jesus remains sitting while he doodles with his fin-
ger in the sand before him. They don't let him off so easily.
They insist. They want an answer. Finally he stands up. He
then looks at the men, some of whom already have stones
in their hands. He says, "Let him who is without sin throw
the first stone." It is silent for a moment. They are caught
by surprise. They had not expected this answer. The oldest
one in the group walks away, dropping his stone alongside
the road. Another one follows him. Then several walk out of
the group at the same time. More and more of them leave,
and finally Jesus is standing there with only the woman,
disheveled, debased, scared to death, and visibly in shock.
He looks at her and asks, "Did anyone condemn you? Did
anyone throw a stone?" She answers, "No, Sir." He then
says, "I won't condemn you either, go home and don't sin
anymore."

Jesus does the same thing to both the woman and the
men. He tells the woman not only to go, but also to change
her life. While she must have loathed herself, standing there
in her shame before Jesus, Jesus touches in her the possibility to be good and do better. He does the same to the
men around her. Why did the oldest one leave first? It might
be that he remembered that he too had sinned; maybe he
too had committed adultery during his life. It might also be
that he reasoned differently. Jesus said, "If any one of you
is without sin—if any one of you is good, just, and righteous—let him throw the first stone." If a person is really
good and righteous, would he be able to take up a stone
and throw it at the soft face, the eye, the head, the breast,
the belly, or the mouth of that woman? He couldn't, could
he? Jesus appealed to the goodness in the men, just as he
did for the woman. They understood, and they left.

ENKINDLING THE DIVINE SPARK

However high the ashes of sins and mistakes are piled in a person's life, Jesus always discovers under those ashes the original fire put there by God. He not only sees it, but he remains faithful to it and tries to rekindle it by blowing new spirit into it. He does what Isaiah foretold he would do:

Forget the former things, do not dwell on the past. See, I am doing a new thing! Now it springs up, do you not perceive it? I am making a way in the desert and streams in the wasteland (Is 43:18).

The healer Jesus finds sufficient divine spark in all of us to activate our healing from within. He is an empowering healer. He does not write off anyone; he is not able to do so. His vision, the same vision Abraham and Sarah began to perceive, did not permit that. Everyone created is charged with the same divine breath, the same fire, the same hope. We all belong to the same reality; it is together that we form the full picture. Jesus did not come only to heal us as individuals. He came to empower everyone to be together. We belong together. We are like pieces in a puzzle. From one piece it is difficult or impossible to see the final picture. It is only when all the pieces are together that the picture shows. We form one family, one city, one kingdom, one offspring, one body, one spirit. Yet we are broken and divided against each other as persons, nations, races, tribes, classes, sexes, generations, in our policies and beliefs. Being a gatherer and an empowering healer in this imperfect world means being at the same time a reconciling peace-maker. Considering Jesus' role, our personal mission and that of our community becomes more and more clear.

For Reflection

1. Share an experience from your life in which someone affirmed you exactly when you needed that affirmation. Have you ever encountered Jesus in such a way?

2. Have you ever empowered someone in a difficult situation?

3. Have you ever been "written off" because of your color, class, education, sex, or religion? How did you react? Did you ever feel you interiorized what those others said to some extent?

4. Frantz Fanon, a West Indian psychiatrist who worked in Algeria during the independence struggle in that North African country, treated both victims and their torturers. He noted that human beings could not begin torturing people before calling them "pigs," "vermin," "dogs," or something similar. Can you explain this? Have you ever encountered such a situation?

CHAPTER 10

Reconciling Peace-Maker

Peace be with you! As the Father has sent me, I am sending you.

(John 20:21)

I t is evening. The disciples are sitting in an upper room in Jerusalem—an upper room is always just a bit safer than a room on the first floor. They have locked the doors. They are scared; and they have good reasons for their fears. Certainly they are worried about the people who condemned Jesus. But they are not too sure about Jesus either. From early in the morning of the third day after Jesus' death and hasty burial, women have come to tell them that they have seen Jesus, that the tomb is empty. Some of them have gone to the tomb to check the women's story. They found the tomb empty, but they did not see Jesus (Lk 24:24). Why hasn't he appeared to them? Has he written them off because of their betrayal? Is it over for them as far as Jesus is concerned?

While they are discussing all this, recounting their stories again and again, Jesus comes. He stands in their midst saying to them, "Peace be with you." To identify himself, he shows his hands and feet. He repeats, "Peace be with you" (Jn 20:20-21). By saying this, he overcomes any feelings of rejection or separation they might have felt. In the same breath Jesus gives them the same task, "As the Father has sent me, I am sending you!"

THE WHOLENESS OF THE KINGDOM

When Jewish scholars finalized the Sacred Scriptures, they did not put the story of Abraham and Sarah at the beginning of their book. Instead, they began with the stories about Adam and Eve. Though different, both stories tell that humanity comes from the same womb, that God created all of us in God's image, that we all live from the same divine breath blown into us, and that we—having the same origin—form one family (Gn 1:26-27). The human family forms, together with God and with the rest of creation, one "piece," and that one piece is called "peace" or "shalom."

All through biblical and human history this wholeness has been threatened. The human family broke the original shalom in its world in many ways. Yet the fundamental unity of creation remains intact. God's Word has not returned in vain. God's work cannot be undone. The vision is never lost. Abram and Sarai—the beginnings of the Jewish people—see it; prophets preach it; Mary expects it; Jesus brings it. This wholeness is the basic nature of the kingdom of God.

This is the dynamic we see at work in the life of Jesus, who simply cannot see anyone as separated from him. Even in his most difficult personal moments he sincerely and with all his heart and mind prays for those who are nailing him to the cross, "Father, forgive them, for they do not know what they are doing" (Lk 23:34). This is the reason Jesus tells us to love our enemies. He does not suggest that we won't have any enemies. He had enemies, and we will have them too, but those enemies belong to the wholeness of the human family.

I tell you, love your enemies and pray for those who
persecute you, that you may be children of your
Father in heaven. He causes the sun to rise on the evil
and the good, and sends rain on the righteous and the
unrighteous (Mt 5:44-45; cf. Lk 6:5).

The unjust, too, relate to God, and God relates to them.
Without that relation they would not even get rain—they
would not be able to exist. It is the same dynamic that
makes Jesus sit down with sinners, prostitutes, tax collec-
tors, children, women, pagans, lepers, and all other disen-
franchised people within his reach. He can't help doing it,
aware as he is of how all relate to God and to each other.
He is referring to the same underlying truth about the
human family when he states:

"Love the Lord your God with all your heart and with
all your soul and with all your mind." This is the first
and greatest commandment. And the second is like it:
"Love your neighbor as yourself" (Mt 22:37-38).

THE LIFE OF COMMUNITY

Luke describes this dynamic as reigning in the Christian
communities throughout the Middle East of his time. Such
communities are composed out of all sorts of people. They
organize an interracial soup kitchen in Jerusalem, an economic revision of the way they own their goods to bridge
the gap between rich and the poor, a fund drive among the
well-to-do in Antioch for the poor in Jerusalem, and reconciling, gathering and peace-making missions to the whole of
their world. The same activities we find today in so many
forms in our own communities, activities that make the
Spirit of Jesus the life principle of the community.
    Luke was not the only one to be impressed by this

aspect of Jesus' dynamic at work. So was Paul. Paul saw reconciliation as the main role Jesus plays in our world and as the reality we have to work out in the world.

All this is from God, who through Christ reconciled us to himself, and gave us the ministry of reconciliation (2 Cor 5:18-20).

Reconciliation here does not mean a simple mutual agreement after a fight or a difficulty. It is about the peace, the wholeness, the shalom Jesus left us. Paul writes that he has only one message, good news hidden up to then. That good news is that we are one:

There is neither Jew nor Greek, slave nor free, male nor female, for you are all one in Christ Jesus (Gal 3:28).

There is no Greek or Jew, circumcised or uncircum-cised, barbarian, Scythian, slave or free, but Christ is all, and is in all (Col 3:11).

Is this the realization of Abram and Sarai's vision, the ful-fillment of Isaiah's prophecies and Mary's hope? It is, and at the same time it is not. The dynamism in our Christian communities, and in our own personal spirituality, is caused by that discrepancy. The reality of our reconciled and restored original oneness has not yet fully unfolded. It is the mystery of the kingdom, which is already here and is not yet here. We are reconciled, we are restored, but the effect of all this has still to be applied in our concrete human situa-tions. Humanity has been breaking the original shalom in this world in many ways, but for God the fundamental unity of creation has never been broken. Jesus lived that original unity of the whole human family and of all creation. He real-ized Abraham and Sarah's vision, the expectation of Isaiah and the other prophets, and he fulfilled the hope of his mother Mary. His followers were not so advanced. Their journey—and ours—is not yet over.

Driven by Jesus' dynamics at work in them, they started the soup kitchen in Jerusalem. His dynamism led them to organize their new ministry to the poor, but within a few weeks they failed. The best of the soup was given to Hebrew widows, while the Gentile ones got the thin of the soup (Acts 6:1). Discrimination crept in. Driven by the same spirit of Jesus they tried to overcome the problem by a reorganization of the service. They chose deacons, with Stephen as their director.

The Corinthians received the good news about their oneness from no one less than Paul. But in no time they had to face up to the fact that they were divided (1 Cor 1:12). They could not even celebrate the breaking of the bread and the sharing of the wine in an orderly way (1 Cor 11:20-23). Paul has to write them to be faithful to the spirit of Jesus.

Even Paul does not succeed in realizing the oneness he preaches. Jesus' dynamic makes him write that men and women are equal, but then he adds, "Women should keep their heads covered and their mouths shut." He notes that the time of masters and slaves is over, yet he states, "Slaves should submit to their masters."

BUT SUCCESS IS ASSURED

Our own communities are full of the same discrepancies. We believe in the unity of all people, and yet in our political and economic structures we hardly take it into account. We confess that all people are equal, yet in our relations to the poor and the wretched in this world that belief often falls flat. Jesus' reconciling peace-making smolders in our hearts, but it seems to get covered under the ashes of personal or communal war and strife.

It is difficult to find a fitting comparison for this tension between the "already" and "not yet" of this shalom, of Jesus' reconciling peace-making, of the kingdom of God. Perhaps it can be compared to a choir wrestling with a difficult piece of music, rehearsing and repeating, failing and trying, stumbling and impatient. The music is there. The singing is not yet what it should be, but because the melody is set and on paper, the stumbling will end and final success is assured.

Others also struggle to express the same reality. A Hindu guru will try to overcome the difference between what is and what is not yet by using the image of the unfolding of a lotus flower. Or the already and not yet of the kingdom can perhaps be compared to what Jacques Rivette, a film maker, once said of a good film, "A film is interesting only if you have this feeling that the film pre-exists and that you are trying to reach it." The essence is in us, and it is not. We have to be helped from outside to find it in ourselves.

Something of the kind happened at Pentecost when the international crowd in the streets of Jerusalem listened to Peter and said, "How is it that we understand what he says each one in his own language?" It was not only that they heard him in their own vernacular or dialect, but that he spoke their language in the sense that they recognized things that now seemed always to have been hidden in the recesses of their own hearts and minds.

Do these examples and analogies help clarify the dynamic tension between the already and not yet of the kingdom of God? Maybe. Jesus struggled with the same difficulty. He left us a multitude of analogies, parables, stories, examples, and signs to express his intentions, his spirit, and his dynamism. Finally, he put his life on the line to bridge the difference, to realize his vision, that vision that had sustained his people from Abraham to his mother Mary.

For Reflection

1. Why did Jesus say:

"When you are bringing your offering to the altar and there remember that your brother or sister has something against you, leave your offering there before the altar, go and be reconciled with your brother or sister first and then come and present your offerings" (Mt 5:23-25)?

2. Is there any reason to stress the peace-making aspects of our mission as Christians in our world? What organizations specialize in this task?

3. Some parishes organize reconciliation or mediation teams to help people avoid legal procedures against each other. Has your Christian community—your family, your religious community, or your parish—ever entered the work of reconciliation? Why? What was the outcome?

4. Comment on Corrie ten Boom's story about meeting after a church service she had led one of the SS guards who had terrorized her in a concentration camp:

He came up to me as the church was emptying, beaming and bowing. "How grateful I am for your message, Fraulein," he said. "To think that as you say, He washed my sins away!" His hand was thrust out to shake mine. And I, who had preached so often to the people in Bloemendaal the need to forgive, kept my hand at my side. Even as the angry, vengeful thoughts boiled through me, I saw the sin of them . . . I prayed, forgive me and help me to forgive him. I tried to smile, I struggled to raise my hand. I could not. I felt nothing, not the slightest spark of warmth or charity. And so again I breathed a prayer. "Jesus, I cannot forgive him. Give me your forgiveness."

As I took his hand the most incredible thing happened. From my shoulder along my arm and through my hand a current seemed to pass from me to him, whole into my heart sprang a love for this stranger that almost overwhelmed me.

And so I discovered that it is not on our forgiveness any more than on our goodness that the world's healing hinges, but on His. When he tells us love our enemies, He gives, along with the command, the love itself.[1]

5. Comment on the following:

Most of the time, we bypass forgiveness. Most of the time . . . we race with lightning speed from our hurts to reconciliation without taking a look at what must be forgiven before lasting healing can take place.[2]

CHAPTER 11

Signs, Symbols, and Reality

Interpret the signs of the times.

(Matthew 16:3)

T he crowds around Jesus constantly asked, "Tell us, when will these things happen? What will be the sign that they are about to be fulfilled?" (Mk 13:4). "Teacher, we want to see a miraculous sign from you!" (Mt 12:8). His disciples also ask at moments when they are alone with him, " 'Tell us,' they said, 'when will this happen, and what will be the sign of your coming and the end of the age?' " (Mt 24:3). Under-standable questions. Jesus promised them the kingdom of God, the year of grace, but not much seemed to happen. Jesus faced the same difficulty. He could point to himself as the fulfillment of the kingdom, but the world at large seemed to remain unchanged. His whole life was a sign of things to come. He overcame in his own life the paradox between the already and not yet of God's reign in a world that still has to overcome that tension.

JESUS—FAITHFUL TO THE VISION

After living thirty years as a carpenter in the village of Nazareth, he heard a voice calling him to be baptized by

John at the River Jordan. The Holy Spirit activated in him the fullness of God's vision for the whole of creation. What Abraham and Sarah had vaguely foreseen, what the prophets had foretold, and what his mother Mary and the group around her had firmly expected, found its fulfillment in him. He fought the temptation to live this fullness only for himself — a temptation any one of us has when discovering a special gift or skill of any significance. He overcame the temptation, came out of the desert, and turned to the others in his world, faithful to the vision. Healing the sick; curing the afflicted; addressing crowds and telling fascinating stories; capturing the attention of thousands and thousands; speaking to women; hailing street children; sitting at table with the rich and the poor; listening to young and old; making the blind see, the deaf hear, the dumb speak, the lame walk; raising the dead; liberating the addicted; returning Lazarus to his family and an only son to a widow; cleaning out the Temple, declaring it a place of prayer for all nations; expressing his amazement at the faith of Jews and Gentiles alike; not only caring for the powerless but empowering them; straightening out the bent-over woman; helping an adolescent girl through her crisis; appreciating and praising the old widow; promoting the human/divine dignity of all; gathering around himself people from all over his world, Jews, Greeks, Romans, and Gentiles of all sorts; praying the Our Father; accepting invitations to banquets and weddings; befriending the outcasts; teaching in synagogues and marketplaces; saving the lives of those harassed; weeping and laughing; forming support groups of twelve, of seventy-two, of hundreds and thousands; meeting people afraid of daylight and publicity in the middle of the night; calming storms and making water blush into wine; organizing outings and picnics; traveling to pagan lands; climbing mountains and hills; going to "the other side"; sailing the sea; and finally, walking to the center of it all — Jerusalem. It was a long journey leading him from the hills of Galilee to the

River Jordan, and on to a hill outside Jerusalem called Golgotha.

The journey led even further. It led to the promised New Jerusalem itself. He laid down his life to attest that he was absolutely sure of the fulfillment of that vision. His willingness to die for his cause in the certainty that he would rise from the tomb is the ultimate and absolute sign he gave. He was willing to die for what he believed in, because he was so sure of God's loving promise that he would not remain dead. His willingness to accept his Passover is his answer to all their pleas for a sign.

> None will be given it except the sign of the prophet Jonah. For as Jonah was three days in the belly of a huge fish, so the son of Man will be three days and three nights in the heart of the earth (Mt 12:39-40; Mt 16:4).

He does not give that answer only once. In both the gospels of Matthew and Luke Jesus gives the answer twice, mentioning the sign of Jonah and applying it to himself. In John's gospel Jesus is more direct. Asked what sign he will give to prove his insight and authority, he speaks of his own body: "Destroy this temple, and I will raise it again in three days" (Jn 2:19). Answering them, he betrays at the same time his exasperation with their blindness to the sign he gave by his life itself by telling them, "A wicked and adulterous generation asks for a miraculous sign!" (Mt 12:39).

JESUS' DYNAMISM

The dynamism in Jesus' life can be explained by his living *here* and *now* the final fulfillment to come. It is more than living ahead of his time. It is living the vision now, at this very moment. It is the dynamism he wants to spark off in his disciples. How could he explain what made his heart burn? How could he explain to those around him that the same love and the consequent reaching out to the New City, the great Gathering, the final Homecoming, the ultimate Healing, the promised Peace and Justice, and the complete Fulfillment could be found within them? How could he rouse in them—from within themselves—the dynamic tension that made him the one he was, is, and always will be? He had to awaken the presence of this dynamism and its effects in the human family.

Jesus' eagerness to make himself understood led to an abundance of creative imagery. The images almost tumble over each other. In the gospels he calls the New Jerusalem that Abraham and Sarah saw, the prophets foretold, and Mary expected, the kingdom of God or the kingdom of heaven. He does that over a hundred times. He compares it to a treasure found in a piece of land. He tells how the finder hid it again, and then, full of joy, went and sold all he had to buy the land with the treasure. The kingdom of God is like a fish swimming in the dark of our subconscious, waiting to be caught and brought into the light of day. It is a pearl found by a merchant, who sells all he has to obtain it. It is like a fishing net thrown out in the ocean and bringing together all its fish. It is like the seed sowed in a field. It is like a tiny mustard seed, which grows into the largest of garden plants. It is like yeast working its way all through a large amount of flour. The one who hears about the kingdom of God is like a householder who brings out of his storeroom new treasures as well as old. The kingdom is like a landowner hiring people to bring in the harvest, a king inviting guests for a feast, a bridegroom waiting for the bride, bridesmaids waiting for the arrival of the bride and bridegroom, a whole party waiting for the wedding party to begin—as Mary once did at Cana!

THE ALREADY AND NOT YET

In those analogies and examples Jesus speaks about a reality that is present—the treasure, the pearl, the fish, the harvest, the seed, the provisions in the pantry. At the same time it is not yet present. It has to be found, dug out, bought, caught, gathered, developed. All these examples point at an already and a not yet! They all indicate a dynamic tension, something to be done, a process spread out over time, a goal to be reached, a journey to be made, a mission to be accomplished. They explain his own dynamism and his own life. They explain why he said of himself—at the peak of his activity—

> "As long as it is day, we must do the work of him who sent me. Night is coming, when no one can work. While I am in the world I am the light of the world" (Jn 9:4-5).

He lived the kingdom to the full in his life; he was the Light. The dynamism that charged his life had to be made active in the whole of the human family. God remained faithful to the original nature of the covenants made between Yahweh and the human family. The outcome would be the result of a process in which both God and humanity continued to be involved. Jesus was not going to take over the process. In him the kingdom of God definitely broke into this world. But humanity would have to join the process to make it its own.

To explain this to people who expected him to start the kingdom of God once and for all among them remained a problem, notwithstanding all his parables and stories. His listeners simply did not understand, or they did not want what he offered. He must have felt especially frustrated at his last gathering with them—the last supper. How could he explain his personal feelings and insights to his confused and mistaken friends during a meal that he knew would be their last one before his Passover?

Just imagine yourself in that situation. Don't be afraid to compare yourself to Jesus. The author of the letter to the

Hebrews wrote that Jesus is "just as we are, except for sin" (Heb 4:15). Remember the story about the woman in front of that burning house in Melbourne, the one who said, "Just put yourself for a moment in their—in this case, in his—position." Just put yourself for a moment in Jesus' position at the last supper. What would you do? We know what he did.

After having washed their feet to show his love and to give them an example of how to relate to each other, he gives a second farewell gesture after the Passover meal is over. In Mark's and in Luke's versions he takes some bread, gives thanks, breaks it, passes it around and says, "Take and eat, this is my body"; he then takes the cup, gives thanks and passes it to his friends, saying, "Drink from it all of you, this is my blood of the covenant that is poured for many" (Mk 14:22-23). In Matthew's gospel Jesus adds to these last words "for the forgiveness of sins" (Mt 26:28). In Luke's version he adds "do this in remembrance of me" (Lk 22:19).

By doing this, Jesus expresses his divine/human love for them. He gives himself to them and for them, and he asks them to do the same. He asks them to *eat and drink him,"* to share his vision and dedication to God's dream for the human family and the whole of creation. He asks them—and us—to live his life, to set out on our journey to the New Jerusalem, healing, gathering, reconciling, and peace-making.

At the last supper Jesus lived the kingdom of God to the full, as he always had done. For a moment his disciples did so as well. When they ate that bread, and drank that wine, they shared in that fullness. They formed the one body, not mystically but really, concretely, though in a sign. During the eucharist the sign of the kingdom of God is at the same time reality and fulfillment. It still is, when we celebrate it. During its celebration we are one body, one blood, one spirit—his body, his blood, his spirit. Every one of us is able to witness to that reality. For a moment the fights are over, the differences healed, the past overcome.

ONE BRIEF GLIMPSE

My most vivid memory of this sharing recalls a Christmas night during the Second World War in the occupied Netherlands. The military commander of the town where I lived lifted the curfew to allow us to go to Midnight Mass. Just before the eucharist a group of German soldiers marched into the church to celebrate with us. No upright Dutch man or woman would ever associate, let alone eat, with them. As kids we stole from them whatever we could, but when they offered us some candy, remembering their own children at home, we would never accept anything, preferring to spit in their faces. At communion time they came to kneel with us at the communion rail — as we did in those days — and nobody objected to those soldiers being there. For a moment all was as it one day will be. We were not enemies. We were interconnected. We were, for a brief moment, at the end of our common journey.

The final gathering, the ultimate reconciliation, the definitive shalom were all realized "already." The future had become real and present just for a moment, just as it always had been in the life of Jesus.

Clearly he didn't just believe in it [the Kingdom of God] or wish for it. He "knew" it, and spoke with the authority that only direct experience can give. For Jesus the absent, the far off had become real and present — present enough for him to stake his life on it.[1]

THE OTHER SIDE OF GOODNESS

Jesus put his life on the line to prove that he was right in his vision, that God guaranteed it. Many of the people under his cross understood that his vision was at stake. They wanted to kill it; they wanted to kill him. It was not the first time they wanted to do this. In his own village they had wanted to kill him two or three years before.

It is not difficult to guess why so many reacted in such a negative way. There is always a kind of "flip side" to any manifestation of goodness, whether it is the goodness of someone like Mother Teresa or the integrity of someone you work with. There is a flip side to the goodness manifest in Jesus too, a serious one, a sinful one. His very goodness can be an obstacle to accepting him. The people who applauded him at his triumphant entry into Jerusalem condemned him some days later. Jesus shows us who we can be, if we want to. He is a challenge to our integrity and to our life — a challenge that is not always and to everyone welcome. He is, as John already wrote, light in our darkness. But not all darkness is willing to accept the light!

That is why they wanted to undo him. They desperately wanted to prove to themselves that he was wrong in his vision and his expectation. It was the only thing they could do to him, their ultimate test. At the peak of his agony he shouted, "My God, my God, why have you forsaken me?" But God did not forsake him or the reality he stood for. He passed the test. Peter was the first one to put into words what happened, when he said at Pentecost:

With the help of wicked men you put him to death, by nailing him to the cross. But God raised him from the dead, freeing him from the agony of death, because it was impossible for death to keep its hold on him (Acts 2:24).

VINDICATION OF A DREAM

Jesus is not the only one vindicated at the moment of his resurrection. So were Abraham and Sarah, in beginning

their journey to the New Jerusalem, the Jerusalem of the
Nations. So were the prophets, with their vision of a kingdom of justice and peace. So was his mother Mary, in her
willingness to give birth to him. So were so many others,
who had been waiting for him. Death did not overcome
what lived in their hearts and their minds. Death could not
overcome the dynamism of God's project, the dynamism
that is present in the communities in which his Spirit lives
on. The Spirit makes him present among us, while he himself is absent. The Spirit lives in the hearts and minds of all
who have a sense of justice, peace, and love, and who
yearn for the newness to come. The Spirit overcomes the
temptation to leave things as they are. The Spirit moves us
on. Jesus himself was tempted to leave things as they were.
He did not give in. He remained faithful to the vision. So
should we.

For Reflection

1. Can you think of any place where the reality of the kingdom of God is transparent in our world? Can you name
   any persons who are examples of this transparency?

2. Do you consider yourself as living a covenant with God?
   If so, what does that mean in your life?

3. Discuss the following story:

   While distributing communion I noticed that one of
   the eucharistic ministers walked away. After some
   time she came back. After the service she asked, "Did
   you see me walking away?" When I answered that I
   had noticed, she told me that she and her teenage
   daughter had had a terrible week. They had offended
   each other and had not spoken since.
      That morning the daughter had stayed in bed when
   the mother came to church. At least that is what she
   thought. But when she was distributing holy commun-

ion, she saw her daughter lining up in front of her to receive the sacrament. Her daughter could have lined up in front of any of the other eucharistic ministers, but she chose her line. When she gave her daughter the host, she was so moved that she began to cry and had to walk away for a while to regain her composure. The eucharist brought them together again.

4. What do you think of the following argument?

   In the '60s a Latin American Catholic priest, Camillo Torres, decided that he could not celebrate the eucharist anymore in a country where people were divided, the rich oppressing the poor, while the church was not willing to tackle this issue. He joined the guerrilla fighters. After having made his decision, he met liberation theologian Gustavo Gutiérrez, who told Camillo that he was not a good theologian, that he misunderstood the significance of the celebration of the eucharist. "In a time like this," Gutiérrez reasoned, "the eucharist is all we have, it is the model of all to come." He apparently did not convince Camillo Torres, who was killed as a freedom fighter some time later.

5. Answer the question at the end of the following quotation: If a person could pass through paradise in a dream, and have a flower presented to him as a pledge that he had already been there, and if he found that flower in his hand when he awoke—'Ay! and what then?[2]

CHAPTER 12

Initiation, Spirit, and Mission

*Go and make disciples of all nations, baptizing
them in the name of the Father, the Son, and of
the Holy Spirit . . . and surely I am with you
always, to the very end of the age.*
                                            (Matthew 28:19-20)

T here are several versions of what happened when
Jesus was baptized by John the Baptist. Matthew
and Mark note that the event occurred "when he
came up out of the water" (Mt 3:16; Mk 1:10).
Luke writes that it happened after his baptism while he was
praying (Lk 3:21). In John's gospel we read that John the
Baptist saw "the Spirit come down from heaven and remain
on him" (Jn 1:32-34). Then there was the voice that said,
"You are my beloved son," indicating God's absolute near-
ness.

REALIZATION OF THE VISION

However and whenever it happened, Jesus' baptism by
John changed his life. It did not change his person, but it
definitely changed his self-awareness—a change so formida-
ble that he needed forty days to get settled and consoli-

dated in this newness. It was an initiation in living the fullness of God's Spirit. Coming out of the desert, he is the presence of God's kingdom in this world. He is the realization of all Abraham and Sarah, the prophets, his mother, Mary, John the Baptist's mother, Elizabeth, and all the poor in spirit, had been hoping and living for. The fullness of the divine dynamism, so openly revealed in him, had to be sparked off in his disciples. They, too, had to find the treasure, the pearl, the fish, the yeast, the salt, the fire, the seed, life, spirit, and God in themselves. They had to see, to hear, to speak, to walk, to smell, and to touch it for themselves. They had to change, to grow up, to turn around, to convert. The kingdom of God had to begin in them, too. To enable them in this was his mission and task, the intention of his life, death, and resurrection. That is why he had come. It was the lesson of all his stories, parables, and examples.

It is also the main topic in the long and repetitive conversations he has with his disciples during the last days of his life. They are upset when he tells them that he is going to leave. What are they going to do without him? He assures them that he will not leave them alone. He insists that it is good for them that he goes. If he doesn't go, they will remain staring at him, like children at their parents. They will never experience and realize that they themselves are empowered by his Spirit. "It is good for you that I go!" (Jn 16:7). He promises them "another advocate," the Holy Spirit, who will be with them while he is physically away (Jn 16:13-15). He assures them that they will be able to do what he himself has been doing and "even greater things than these" (Jn 14:12).

THE VISION WITHIN US

What happened to Jesus during his baptism by John should happen to us during our baptism. That is what he meant when he told his disciples that they would be baptized with the Holy Spirit (Acts 1:5). He wants us to do what he did. He wants us to share in his experience of the Holy Spirit, who always had been present in his life but became visible to all after his baptism. We have to help others share in what Jesus himself experienced in his own life, the realization that the divine longing for the justice, peace, and love of the kingdom of God is living in all and everyone. He put this experience in words when he prayed with his disciples, "Our Abba in heaven . . . your kingdom come, your will be done" (Mt 6:9). This prayer introduced a new covenant between God and humanity.

OUR MISSION—TOGETHER

The disciples are charged with a mission, his mission. They are sent as he was sent (Jn 20:21). They had to begin in the whole of the world what he had begun in them by his deeds and his words (Jn 15:3). They are to help others flush out in themselves their deepest longing, the treasure, the pearl, their value, their worth, their dignity, their center, the kingdom of God—the vision. At the end of the gospel of Matthew Jesus makes that mission explicit at his last meeting with them before he ascends to heaven:

Go and make disciples of all nations, baptizing them in the name of the Father, the Son, and of the Holy Spirit (Mt 28:19).

The whole of the human family has to be initiated in the reality that all have one and the same divine Parent, that we are created in one and the same Offspring, and that we are all vivified by one and the same Spirit. The Trinitarian formula Matthew reports tells us about the life of God. It tells us also how God relates to us and how we relate to God.

Anyone among us is of divine origin (Gn 1:27). We are all created together as God's offspring in the Son (Jn 1:1-4); we are living from the same divine Spirit breathed in us from the beginning (Gn 2:7). It is a relationship that not only defines us, but it is at the same time a reality we have to work out in our world. As Catholic African President Julius Nyerere of Tanzania once said:

> We say the human being was created in the image of God. I refuse to imagine a God who is miserable, poor, ignorant, superstitious, fearful, oppressed and wretched. If a human being is really the temple of God, we have to do something about the flies in the eyes of a child, as those flies are ruining God's temple.[1]

The baptismal formula is—like the eucharistic breaking of the bread and sharing of the wine—an action program. It is a political issue. It is an economic task. It is a spiritual issue. It is a social plan. It is the charter of the kingdom of God. It is what empowers us. It is the reality Jesus lived in his life. It is the kind of life he led his disciples to discover in themselves. It is the life he asked them to witness to in such a way that others would feel it vibrate within them too. It is the kingdom of God in and among us. It is a life to be actualized in everyone. It is the reason we are equipped with his Spirit:

> What was once preached by the Lord, or what was once wrought in Him for the saving of the human race, must be proclaimed and spread abroad to the ends of the earth (Acts 1:8), beginning from Jerusalem (cf. Lk 24:47). Thus, what He once accomplished for the salvation of all may in the course of time come to achieve its effect in all.
> To accomplish this goal, Christ sent the Holy Spirit

from the Father. The Spirit was to carry out His saving work inwardly and to impel the Church toward her proper expansion. Doubtless, the Holy Spirit was already at work in the world before Christ was glorified. Yet on the day of Pentecost, He came down upon the disciples to remain with them forever (cf. Jn 14:16). On that day the Church was publicly revealed to the multitude, the gospel began to spread among the nations by means of preaching, and finally there occurred a foreshadowing of that union of all peoples in a universal faith.[2]

THE ORIGINS OF MISSION

Jesus gave us that assignment. But we aren't only "in mission" because Jesus commanded it. There is another dynamism at work—the dynamism of people who are aware of the Spirit of Jesus in themselves and in their communities. To be "charged" with Jesus' Spirit means being taken up in a process, a process of a cross-cultural gathering of all the nations and the whole of creation, a process that reaches from the vision of Abraham and Sarah to the fulfillment at the end of time.

When the Second Vatican Council began to discuss mission, the participants were given a working paper that had been prepared for them. It spoke about the "apostolic origin of Mission." The council did not accept this description of mission as starting with the apostles. The true origin of mission goes far back beyond the apostles to the old covenants with Moses, Abraham and Sarah, Noah, and Adam and Eve. It reaches back into the depths of the divine life. It is rooted and grounded in the heart of every single human being. It might be hidden, it might be swimming in the dark, but it is there.

When Jesus prays at the last supper "that they all may be

one," he adds "just as you are in me, and I am in you" (Jn 17:21). Mission does not concern only Jesus Christ; it goes back to the creative and loving process of the three Persons in the Blessed Trinity. Mission describes a life we all share, the purpose of the church, a process in which Jesus played a decisive role here on earth.

> The Mission of the Church is not derived in the first place from humanity's need of salvation; its primary source is in God self, who as Living Love, has an inner necessity to give self. Like Jesus, and in the spirit of Jesus, the Church lives by this divine compulsion. Seen in this way, mission is not so much the Church's task as an expression of her very being, God is self-giving love. The Church is the fruit of this love, and can only be herself when she brings it to expression by what she is, before she embarks on any works or enterprises.
>
> The necessity of mission flows from the very nature of the Church, willed by God to carry out the mission of the Son under the impulsion of the Holy Spirit. . . . *All Christians have within them a dynamism directed towards this end. This dynamism is nothing other than the action of the love of God within them, oper-ating by the Spirit* (emphasis added).[3]

Mission is a process all of us are engaged in when we are faithful to the divine-human dynamism at work in ourselves, being—like him—gatherers, reconcilers, peacemakers, empowerers, and healers, and at the same time, willing to be gathered, reconciled, empowered, and healed ourselves. And this leads to the second part of this book.

For Reflection

1. We usually don't think of the Trinity as Parent, Offspring, and Spirit. Do those titles help shed light on our relation with God and with others? Discuss.

2. There are different forms of baptism: by pouring water over the head or by total immersion in water. Those different forms lead to different explanations. Pouring water over the head leads to the idea of cleansing; baptism by immersion calls up the image of going with Jesus from death to life through the tomb. Which form do you prefer? Why?

3. Baptism is an initiation rite. Though we have initiation rites in our society, it is in older societies that we can find them in all their significance.

    For example, many African societies initiate boys and girls into adult life when they reach the age and the physical maturity to marry. Both boys and girls go through a ceremony—a rite of passage—in which they undergo some bodily hardship to introduce them to the rigor and discipline of adult life. This initiation into adulthood indicates that life as a child is over. One ethnic group circumcises them, another tattoos their faces, a third pierces their ears. Those rites do not make the young people physically able to be mothers or fathers. Their bodily growth has already taken care of that. However, they were not allowed to *function* as such before being initiated. Their initiation formalizes and actualizes their bodily maturity.

    Does presenting baptism as an initiation rite help explain what happens during baptism?

4. In a talk given at Woodstock College in 1966 biblical scholar Raymond Brown is reported to have said, "The Holy Spirit is the presence of Jesus when Jesus is absent." What do you think of that statement?

5. Would the followers of Jesus Christ have engaged in mission even if he had not ordered them explicitly to do so? Explain.

Part II

FANNING THE FLAME

CHAPTER 13

Our Mission: Challenges and Priorities

That all of them, Father, may be one, just as
you are in me and I in you.

(John 17:21)

P eople attentive to the Spirit in them don't need Jesus' command in order to engage in his mission. God's loving Spirit will move them. The same impelling force made Abraham and Sarah leave their home and enabled Moses to lead his people. The Spirit inspired the scribes to tell the story of Eve and Adam, the prophets to write their visions, and Mary to accept her child, Jesus. The same dynamism made Jesus live, die, and rise. Those key figures and many others — too many to name or even to count — engaged in a world to which we are now the heirs. Now it is our turn to move on, to gather, and to heal. We know and feel that. We too share the vision of the New Jerusalem. As one of the most forceful statements of the Second Vatican Council tells us:

The joys and the hopes, the grief and the anxieties of the people of this age, especially those who are poor or in any way afflicted, these too are the joys

and hopes, the griefs and anxieties of the followers
of Christ. Indeed, nothing genuinely human fails to
raise an echo in their hearts. For theirs is a community of human beings. United in Christ they are led
by the Holy Spirit, in their journey to the Kingdom
of their Father, and they have welcomed the news of
salvation which is meant for every human being.
That is why this community realizes that it is truly
and intimately linked with the human family and its
history.[1]

FAILING IN MISSION

It is a pity that this text speaks about us in the third person: "United in Christ, *they* are led . . ." It would have been
better to speak about ourselves in the first person: "United
in Christ, *we* are led . . ." The text speaks about us, about
all of us. Who among us has not sighed upon seeing the
many human conflicts in our world? Those clashes change
from place to place and from time to time, yet they can be
found all over the world all the time. At the present time
parts of Europe, Asia, Africa, and South America are
involved in bloody civil war and unrest. The cities in many
Western nations are divided between the poor and the rich.
Drugs, gang wars, and street robberies keep the old and the
young out of the streets and the parks. The youngest and
the oldest — always the most vulnerable in any society — are
repeatedly neglected and abused. Families are disintegrat-
ing. Individuals find it increasingly difficult to maintain their
moral integrity, self-worth, and meaning. The old dream of
Abraham and Sarah, the prophecy of so many prophets, the
readiness of Mary to serve, and Jesus' death and resurrection seem irrelevant. The old song of the good news is
rarely heard and hardly distinguishable in all the noise and
uproar.

Yet the good news is the melody Pope John Paul II sang in a long encyclical on mission entitled *Redemptoris Missio* (*The Redeemer's Mission*), which was published in 1991. The "song line" is something of a lament. The author is clearly upset. *Redemptoris Missio* is the letter of someone who is convinced that he, and the church he is shepherding, are failing. He writes about "an undeniable negative tendency" and about the fact that "specific missionary activity is waning." Anyone aware of the actual situation would have written in that tone. We *are* failing. Explaining to himself—and his readers—where we fall short, the pope alludes, as Jesus did, to that pervasive vision:

"That they all may be one . . . so that the world may believe that you have sent me" (Jn 17:21).

We neglect to work toward the oneness Jesus prayed for in the last hours before his death and resurrection. But it is our mission to work at answering that prayer. If we help to make the whole of humanity realize that we are one divine/human family, we will be not only the carriers of good news, but we will be a divine blessing to all. If we manage to do that in Jesus' name, all will see him as the one sent by God. It is interesting to note the order in that quotation, which comes in John's gospel straight from the mouth of Jesus. We should work at that "oneness," so that people will believe in Jesus, and not the other way round! We should *first* show what it is all about, and only then drop the name, as Peter did when he worked his first miracle!

REASONS FOR SADNESS

There are several reasons Pope John Paul II is in a special and personal way sensitive to the sadness of our situation. He has traveled the world as no pope ever did before. Those pilgrimages to local churches have confronted him with human division and sin, war and hunger, lack of respect for human rights and discrimination, squalor and injustice, sickness and powerlessness, and the fact that masses of people have never even heard Jesus' name. All over the world he has heard the cries of those lost in their material poverty and of others lost in their riches.

There is another reason why all this deeply affects him. As a young man he lived for years in utter poverty. His father starved to death during the Second World War. He himself was chased away from the university where he was studying, because the Nazi occupiers considered the Poles an inferior race, not fit to study at a university. They were destined only to serve human beings superior to them. He did forced labor in a quarry and later in a dye factory. He knows from bitter personal experience what it means when one's human dignity is not respected and God's message about humanity is disregarded.

John Paul II is clearly upset because we don't work sufficiently at Jesus' priority. But there is another reason. Again, it is a reason any one of us might have found out for himself or herself. It is the difficulty of our task. Humanity comprises a great variety of human beings, peoples, cultures, religions, and ideologies. In this century, with its devastating and lasting world conflicts, we have begun to experience how different and unequally the parts of the earth relate to one another. Anthropologists, sociologists, economists, political scientists, politicians, philosophers, educators, and journalists agree that bringing humanity together asks for a total change of heart and mind—a conversion—from all of us. Convergence will be difficult because of the different approaches we have developed over the ages. The oneness of the vision, *"e pluribus unum"* ("out of many one") is far from realized.

It will find full expression only in the realization of the gospel message of the kingdom of God.

SEEKING THE VISION

Pope John Paul II refers to that fullness with a reference to Abraham and Sarah. He reminds us of the divine/human vision first seen by Abram and Sarai. Yahweh promised this couple that they, and "all the clans" of the earth going their way, would be blessed (Gn 12:3).[2] Pope John Paul II notes that the final homecoming of the human family is God's dream and God's plan, and that it found its full expression in Jesus. "Jesus himself is the good news . . . not just by what he says or does, but by what he is."[3] He expressed God's promised future in his love for everyone, friends and enemies alike, and especially for those religiously, socially, or economically neglected and marginalized.

According to its shepherd, the church falls short. We are not sufficiently engaged in our empowering, healing, reconciling, and peace-making task. We are not gathering in what Jesus himself called the human harvest. We even fail to proclaim the good news to those who have never heard it. If we fail to work at our mission, the realization of our divine/human oneness, we are no help to the human family. We aren't responding to Jesus' ideal, and our worship is failing. We are not forming the house of the Lord, and we are not building a real home for the human family either. We are in danger of being only a kind of sectarian group shelter. And a shelter for only some is in the end a shelter for no one at all. We risk not helping to fulfill God's dream and humanity's own deepest yearning.

THE PRACTICE OF MISSION

The encyclical is especially dedicated to the proclamation of the good news to those who have never heard it. It is

about the need to go to the unevangelized, a work missionaries or missioners, male and female, clerical and lay, have
been doing all through the history of the Christian community. There is good reason for the pope to address this
issue. The numbers of persons involved in that work is
steadily declining.

John Paul II does not restrict mission to this going out to
the unevangelized. Mission requires more than proclamation. Our mission is not accomplished at the moment that
the kingdom has been announced; it must be put into practice. The letter speaks about the mission and the work of
those baptized *in the world in which they live.* It insists on
the need of ecumenical contacts with other Christian
denominations. It mentions those who once were Christians,
but are no longer, and who have to find again "The Way" —
as the first communities in the Acts of the Apostles often
called their Christian lifestyle.

In everyday life these different tasks and interests go
together. We can't do one without the other. We will only be
able to bring the human family together if we reach out to
those far away. It is the example Jesus gave on his endless
trips to the other side of the lake and to the foreign areas in
his own neighborhood. We have to contact people and talk
to them. We have to *dialogue.* We — and they — have to
respect in the others their roots, their history, their inspiration, and the seeds God sowed in them from all eternity.
This kind of contact will only make sense if our own community is hope-giving, inspiring, and attractive to them.

"AT HOME" IN THE HOUSE OF THE LORD

It is useless to proclaim the kingdom of God if we are
not building it in our own communities. We have to be seen
as people who are at work at the kingdom of God, a reign
of justice, equality, and peace. We must be people who not

only have the signs and symbols of the one body and the one spirit, but who also are seen trying to realize it in our personal and communal lives. We have to welcome the ones we reach in a way that makes them feel at home with us. We are accustomed to do things in our way; they have their ways. Yet they should feel just as "at home" in the house of the Lord as we do. We will be able to learn a lot from each other. We will enrich each other. We will be surrounding Jesus with our personal and communal gifts, just as John foresaw in Revelation (Rv 21:24). Yet creating this common home will have its unavoidable problems.

It would be difficult to organize this "being at home with the Lord and each other" ideal from the center or from above. It can only come from within those communities themselves. They should be able to sit at the feet of the Lord in their own circle.

If we want to be carried by God's love and vision for humanity and creation, if we want to work at the mission Jesus left us, if we want to be faithful to his spirit in us, if we want to continue the journey Abram and Sarai, Mary and Elizabeth, and so many others began, then our priorities are clear. We are engaged in a gathering, empowering, liberating, healing, reconciling, and peace-making process. This process is not the exclusive task of missionaries or any group in the church, but the task of the whole church, of the people of God. Gathering into the kingdom of God asks for proclamation and dialogue, justice and peace, empowerment and liberation, incarnation and inculturation. All those terms sound lofty and abstract, but their reality touches our daily life. They were the warp and the woof of Jesus' life. And they are the interwoven topics of the next chapters.

For Reflection

1. What conclusion would you draw from the following report by a missionary sister in Lebanon?

I was appointed for mission work in Lebanon. I taught
at a local school. One of my tasks was to prepare
children and adults for baptism. I like teaching and
introducing Jesus in that way. It was not the only
thing I had to do. We had no water in the house in
which I lived together with some other sisters. We
took turns fetching water at a tap some miles from
our house. The water supply consisted of that one
tap, standing alongside the road in a field. It ran only
an hour or so in the morning. The timing was uncer-
tain. You had to go there early to be sure to catch it.
At about nine in the morning a lot of people, mainly
women, assembled around the tap. Most of them
were local Muslim women. Being American made me
really stick out in the crowd. We began talking to one
another. One day a woman said: "You are from America aren't you? There is plenty of water there, why are
you here sitting waiting for it?" I explained to her that
it was my love for Jesus and for them that brought
me there. She was intrigued by my answer, and I suddenly understood what "mission by presence" means.

2. "People today put more trust in witnesses than in teach-
   ers" (*Redemptoris Missio*, no. 43). Do you agree?

3. The liturgical committee in a parish is preparing for
   Christmas. One group of parishioners would like to use
   an advent wreath, another group a picture of Our Lady
   of Guadalupe. What do you think? What would you say/
   do?

4. Have you ever proclaimed Jesus? How did you do it? Or,
   why did you choose not to do so?

CHAPTER 14

How to Proclaim and Dialogue

Were not our hearts burning within us while he talked with us on the road, and opened the Scriptures to us?

(Luke 24:32)

All of us have been confronted by people who have tried to force their religious convictions on us. They might have been followers of the Reverend Moon, Hare Krishna chanters, Latter Day Saints, Witnesses of Jehovah, or followers of Jesus Christ. They stand on a soapbox on the corner of a street in Nairobi. They approach us in their black suits in front of the Royal Palace in Amsterdam. They sing their hymns in the market at Brixton in London. They raise their prophetic voice on the steps of the Capitol in Washington, D.C. They might sit next to us in a bus or a plane. We meet them at the front door of our house. Their messages are different, but their approach is the same. They have the truth, and we don't. They assure us that they have the answer for us, though they don't ask for our questions. They proclaim their beliefs without fear or hesitation. There is no need, they say, for any dialogue. You believe, or you don't. You belong to the saved ones, or you are lost. Is this the approach for the followers of Jesus? After all, they must have some success, or they wouldn't continue.

When questioned about their approach, they often answer that Jesus commanded them to "go to the ends of the earth, preach and baptize in the name of the Father, the Son and the Holy Spirit." This is indeed an order we received. There is, however, more to our mission than just that order.

RESONATING TO THE VOICE WITHIN

Mary, Jesus' mother, did not obey and submit only because Yahweh spoke to her through an angel. She listened to God speaking to her from outside, of course, but she was also charged with God's Spirit and God's dream within herself. When Jesus tells his disciples in the end of the gospel of Matthew to "Go!"[1] he adds, "I am with you always, until the end of the world" (Mt 28:20). That is the reason they do what they do on their mission. It comes from within themselves; it is Jesus' Spirit in them that they feel compelled to proclaim. From within themselves they know and feel that the human family has to be gathered, that justice and peace should be pursued, that creation has to be respected, and that God's kingdom should be realized.

These inner dynamics are found not only in the disciples of Jesus, but in all human beings. God's breath has been blown into all of us! Pope John Paul II put it in this way:

In proclaiming Christ to non-Christians, the missionary is convinced that, through the working of the Spirit, there already exists in individuals and peoples an expectation, even if an unconscious one, of knowing the truth about God, about humanity, and about how we are set free from sin and death. The missionary's enthusiasm in proclaiming Christ comes from the conviction that he is responding to that expectation.[2]

The North American bishops implied the same presence of the Spirit in the native peoples of the United States when they wrote:

> The story of the coming of the faith to our hemisphere must begin, then, not with the landing of the first missionaries, but centuries before with the history of the Native American peoples.[3]

A person does not need Jesus to value justice, integrity, peace, and love. The disciples were attracted by Jesus because in Jesus they saw those values *in their fullness*. Meeting Jesus, they suddenly saw who they were destined to be.

Some examples from everyday life may help clarify this notion. Perhaps you remember a time that you wanted to express your love, but you felt a bit shy about it. Maybe you wrote a letter, then tore it up because the words were just not right. Or you picked up the telephone and dialed your beloved, but hung up before the phone was answered. The words simply did not come. Then you found a book, just by chance. A book full of poems. One of them was a love poem that expressed exactly what you wanted to say. Suddenly all your thoughts and feelings fell in place.

Another example is music. Most of us are filled with the beginnings of melodies, rhythms, and beats. They sometimes come out under a shower, or while driving a fast car on a clear day. They remain bits and pieces until suddenly, at a concert, a jazz session, or just listening to the radio it is as if you have heard it before. The saxophone in the jazz band expresses your deepest feelings, or the popular song frees your heart!

As a final example, a scientist might have all kinds of hints and hunches, beginnings of theories, vague models, and intuitions. Then suddenly he or she discovers one new piece of information, sees something in a new light, and it all falls in place.

It is this role Jesus plays in the life of many. He attracts us because there are in all of us ideas and dreams, imaginations and realities, intuitions and inspirations.

JESUS' STORY IS FOR EVERYONE

Jesus is no stranger to anyone. We shouldn't announce him as a stranger when we tell his story to others. In his recent writings Pope John Paul II stressed several times that Jesus Christ is connected with each human individual.[4] It is in this connection that we find the need and the possibility of a dialogue with others.

It is pointless to begin an exchange by saying what *we* believe about Jesus and all he lived, died, and rose for. Others must discover for themselves that Jesus is the Way, the Truth, and the Life. Our role is to open a dialogue in which *we* tell the story of Jesus, open the books about him, so to speak, to help others discover *for themselves* who he is. Jesus himself used this method when he met the travelers on the road to Emmaus the day of his resurrection. He did not tell them who he was; rather, he told his story and left it to them to recognize him.

Evangelization and dialogue go together. When I tell the story of Jesus, I proclaim the good news of the kingdom of God, and the listeners will respond from within their own experience. Then we can dialogue. And when I dialogue with someone on these matters, I hardly can avoid speaking in terms of the good news. Which means that in one way or another I am proclaiming it. God's Spirit in me finds its counterpart in the same Spirit in them.

For some time it has been the custom to call the "others" in our dialogue anonymous Christians. To do that is no help. It creates difficulties in our communication. It seems to appropriate the people we dialogue with. We all know from our own personal experience how awkward it is when others tell us, "I know what you think." No one ever knows that. People have to define themselves. Remember what my African colleague told me about telling a story! We can say, however, that we are both taken up in the same process, that we in our dialogue are pilgrims on the way to our common fulfillment! Our dialogue can begin with the gathering and healing story of Jesus.

MEETING GOD AMONG "OTHERS"

Missionaries often say that they learned more from the people they went to than they taught them. This learning is sometimes called *mission in reverse*. It means that those missionaries would like to let their home churches profit from the riches they found among those they went to. We *all* learn in a dialogue on God and on kingdom of God affairs.

It is thrilling to look at children playing or professional athletes breaking records. It is intriguing to read about human feelings and sentiments or to look at films about them. But it can be more exhilarating to share in the life of God in others. Jesus experienced this himself dialoguing with Samaritans and with the Syro-Phoenician woman, a Roman officer, and so many others. Their faith and insight amazed him. Our contacts with others often will amaze us too. Father Vincent Donovan, a missionary among the Masai in the Great Rift Valley in East Africa, called the book about his experiences there *Christianity Rediscovered*.[5] Father Christian van Nispen, a Jesuit who lives and works in Cairo, Egypt, once said at a meeting of specialists in the Muslim-Christian dialogue that the church discovers Jesus when she reaches out to others, as Jesus himself crosses all borders to reveal himself to others.[6] Practically anyone who seriously shares the faith experiences of "others" discovers God is there. Pope Paul VI opted for this approach when he said:

The Catholic Church looks further in the distance . . . beyond the Christian horizon. For how can she put limits to her love if she should make her *own* the love of God our Father, *Who rains down His grace on all alike* (Mt 5:46) and who loved so the world as to give for it His only begotten Son (John 3:16)? *She looks then beyond her own domain* and sees those other religions which maintain the concept of one God, creator, sustainer, sovereign, and transcendent, who worship God with sincere acts of piety, and *whose beliefs and practice are the founding principles of their moral and social life.* . . . She cannot help speaking, to assure them of the *esteem the Catholic Church has for all there is in them of truth, goodness and of the human* (emphasis added).[7]

We should not overlook some common human difficulties in this kind of dialogue. All of us have the tendency to be jealous of what we have and who we are. When speaking about something as personal and delicate as our relation to God and God's relation to us, that jealousy may creep in. Like young lovers, we tend to think that our relationship is unique, that no one loves as we do.

We need to keep in mind that *all* of us are gifted in our own way by the same Father, all of us are created together in the same Son, all of us are enlivened by the same Spirit. All of us are equipped from within to organize ourselves better while living and worshiping together here on this planet Earth. It is together that we are on our way to the New Jerusalem, our heavenly home in which there are — Jesus assured us — many rooms (Jn 14:2). And we should thank God for that information!

FAILURES IN INTERRELIGIOUS DIALOGUE

All through history the human family has been discussing religious and ideological issues. Interreligious dialogue is part and parcel of human history, often in very violent forms.

One day I took the metro in Washington, D.C. At the ticket machine someone gave me a pamphlet. I was busy and didn't pay any attention to what it was until I sat down in the train. It read in big print: "Jesus is the Messiah." The person next to me glanced at the text. Then he looked at me and said: "Do you believe that? They murdered us in Christian Europe, you know." This is a typical Jewish reaction to the Christian belief that in Jesus the Messiah appeared here on earth. They comment that Christians must be very naive to believe that the world as it is at the moment is a saved one. This is a reaction we have to take seriously when speaking too triumphantly about Jesus being the answer. We Christians believe that in Jesus the kingdom of God broke through in this world. Equipped with his Spirit we should be better at working at its justice and peace. As long as we haven't ended our task, it is a good thing that the Jews keep the ancient Judaic expectation alive. It helps the church to rethink the relationship between Christianity and Judaism.

A similar unfortunate historical relationship exists among Judaism, Christianity, and Islam. In the seventh century Mohammed hoped that either the Jews or the Christians of his region would be willing to help him in the emancipation of his Arab people. When both religious bodies showed no interest, he reconsidered his position and reasoned that both Jews and Christians were no longer faithful to Abram and Sarai's vision of all nations climbing the mountain of the Lord. Both Christians and Jews, he reasoned, had betrayed that original and foundational revelation. He told his followers to change the direction of their prayer mats toward Mecca, where Abram and Sarai built their house. He argued that he had to rally humanity in a new human/divine *umma* or family because the others had failed.

Karl Marx, a Jew who was baptized as a child, blamed the

Jewish, Christian, and Muslim religious institutions alike for their lack of interest in social justice and human dignity issues. Seeing their belief in God as the reason for this neglect, he wanted to bring "God's" kingdom about here on earth without any belief in God at all. It simply did not work.

. . . AND SUCCESSES

The Asian religions and Christianity have been influencing and often stimulating each other since contact was made centuries ago. Mohandas Gandhi was not only influenced by the teachings and the life of Jesus, but he in his turn influenced Christians of different denominations like Peter Maurin and Dorothy Day of *The Catholic Worker*, Danilo Dolci in Italy, Jacques Maritain and Lanza del Vasto in France, Cesar Chavez, Thomas Merton, and Martin Luther King, Jr., all of whom traced their vision to the teachings of Jesus. Yet they all acknowledged that it was by meeting the Hindu Gandhi, and not through the teaching of the Christian churches, that they met the nonviolent face of Jesus.[8]

LEARNING FROM "OTHERS"

We are surrounded by believers who do not go to church anymore. It is not that they are not religious. On the contrary. They seem to have outgrown their church communities. They hope to quench their religious thirst and solve their religious problems in what they call New Age Religion. They claim that their former church leaders never told them what they discovered since they left their churches. It was in their contacts with others that they discovered a divine spark within themselves. Either nobody ever told them before, as Christians, about the Spirit who dwells in all of us, or nobody told them in a way they could understand. In our dialogue with them we might learn a lot about ourselves and our own religious needs.

It is in our contacts with all those "others," their old and new beliefs, that we discover the ramifications of the risen humanity, how we belong together and complement each other religiously and spiritually. So much remains hidden in us, so many possibilities and potentialities remain undiscovered if we stand solely on our own. It is as if God sowed his goods in all of us in different ways. We are pieces of God's gigantic jigsaw puzzle, a puzzle Jesus came to bring together. It is in him that we have the full picture. But we have to tell each other our stories in order to find in each other what in its fullness is found in Jesus.

Dialogue should not only be at the heart of our contact with the Spirit in others, it also should be revived in our Christian circle. The reformation churches formed themselves in protest against perceived and real abuses. They meant to amend and correct existing administrative and spiritual mismanagement and imbalances. Some stressed, and sometimes over-stressed beliefs and attitudes that were under-stressed or neglected by others. Still, Christians of the different denominations are historically and dialectically intertwined. While in their devotion and ecclesial set-up some pay especial attention to God as Parent of all, others prefer to stress their personal adhesion to Jesus Christ, God's Son and Offspring. Still others prefer to revel enthusiastically in the presence of God's Spirit within them. We cannot understand ourselves without contacting the others. We should seriously engage our differences, bringing together all that is good and true.

DIALOGUE WITHIN THE CHURCH

The same dynamic is found in the Roman Catholic Church. Since the Second Vatican Council we live in a church that has different approaches to the same mysteries. The Vatican II documents so often give different and complementary definitions of one and the same truth and reality. It is in those tensions between old and new that we find inspiration and life in a true dialogue. Didn't Jesus tell us that the disciples of the kingdom of heaven will bring new treasures as well as old out of his storeroom (Mt 13:52)?

CONDITIONS FOR FRUITFUL DIALOGUE

To make interreligious, interdenominational, and inter-church dialogue successful, or even possible, some conditions have to be fulfilled — conditions that flow from the nature of the exchange. The dialogue must be between what Jesus made vibrate in us and what is resonating with God's Spirit in the others. It is there that we find our contact point and our inspiration to go further in our common journey to our final destination. This means that God's Spirit must be active in all partners. They must be in contact with God's presence in them. A prayerful being present to God is thus presupposed as a first condition.

We read in Luke's description of Jesus' baptism by John that Jesus is at prayer when the Spirit in the form of a dove descends on him and the voice is heard. In the Acts of the Apostles we read that the apostles prayed before any mission or "proclaiming dialogue" was undertaken. It is only from that contact point that a fruitful dialogue can start, and the willingness to really listen to each other can begin. Without that touching point with the Spirit in us, we won't be able to do anything at all. We begin by prayerfully relying on God's presence in us and in them, until we both realize how nice it might be to converse with and about God, revealing to each other the treasure we carry in ourselves. And we discover that treasure in ourselves at the same time, because that is how those faith exchanges work out!

Two other conditions have to be fulfilled. We need a double faithfulness.[9] We have to be faithful to ourselves, and we have to be faithful in listening to the others. As Pope Paul VI writes:

> Fidelity both to the message whose servants we are, and to the people to whom we must transmit it safe and sound is the central axis of Evangelization (no. 4).[10]

Dialogue has often been begun by individuals, or by some representatives of the different religious groups. In the case of the Catholic-Jewish dialogue it has led to considerable results. But it is a task that cannot be left to individuals alone. Faith communities should get involved. Taking up this ministry as a community effort is still called "The Wild Card," but as the author who gave it that name, David A. Bos, wrote, it might well go down as a new chapter in the history of mission.[11]

ADDITIONAL AREAS FOR DIALOGUE

As we live together in a world that on the whole is far from realizing the kingdom, and consequently far from ideal, there are many other concerns we have in common. One insight all religious believers and all non-religious thinking human beings alike express is the need to do something about this world socially, economically, politically, and environmentally. This calls for an additional dialogue, one that can be shared even by those who do not choose to join our interreligious dialogue. For them this will be the test of our religious sincerity. If, as followers of Jesus, we confess to believe in a God who is the Parent of all, who sent his Offspring into this world, and who together with that Offspring sends the Spirit into everyone, how can we not be busy with clearing those social and ecological issues? His companions from Emmaus did not recognize Jesus while he was opening the scriptures to them. Afterward they told each other that their hearts had been burning during that explanation. Yet they had not recognized him at the time. They discovered who he was at table, when he took their bread and broke it for them, sharing it in the way they had heard he did at his last supper before his death. Which leads us into the heart of the next chapter.

For Reflection

1. Have you ever prayed with non-Catholics? with non-Christians? Form a delegation in your parish or community to visit a neighboring non-Catholic community or to visit a synagogue, mosque, or temple. (Ask before whether you will be welcome.) Invite the community to one of your services.

2. Comment on the following quotations:

   The history of Judaism did not end with the destruction of Jerusalem, but rather went on to develop a religious tradition (Vatican City, 1975).[12]

   Our common spiritual heritage is considerable. Help in better understanding certain aspects of the Church's life can be gained by taking an inventory of that heritage, but also by taking into account the faith and religious life of the Jewish people as professed and lived now as well (Pope John Paul II, 1982).[13]

   There is the affirmation about Christ and his saving event as central to the economy of salvation — an affirmation which is essential to the Catholic Faith (Section 1, #7). This does not mean that the Jews as a people cannot and should not draw salvific gifts from their own traditions. Of course, they can and should do so (Jorge Mejia, 1985).[14]

3. How do you react to the following opinion?

With the remarks of Paul VI at the opening of the second session of the Second Vatican Council Paul VI began the movement from talking *about* other religions, and talking *to* other religions, to dialogue *with* other religions and with these other religions *about itself.* Pope Paul sought to move the Church in the direction of appreciating and learning from other religions, while simultaneously offering her own spiritual treasures to them.[15]

4. This chapter stressed the need for prayer as a condition for fruitful interreligious dialogue. Can you explain why? Would a meditation on the Our Father be a help in this context? Why?

CHAPTER 15

The Why and How of Justice, Peace, and Creational Integrity

*See what this godly sorrow has produced in
you: what earnestness, what eagerness to clear
yourselves, what indignation, what alarm, what
longing, what concern, what readiness to see
justice done.*

(2 Corinthians 7:11)

I t was early in the evening. It was dark outside in
Nairobi, Kenya, East Africa; it is always dark by
seven in the evening. The only noises were the
traffic in the distance and the crickets nearby. It
had been a busy day at the office of the university chapel.
Many visitors had come to ask for help, help that often was
not available. I was tired and relieved that the office was
closed. I entered the presbytery. Someone must have been
waiting, because immediately afterward there was a knock
at the front door. I opened the door, and a man asked for
some food. I said, "Sorry, I can't help you. You are too late.
The office is closed," and locked the door in his face. There
was another knock at the door. I pretended not to hear it.
The knocking continued. I finally opened the door. The
same man was there, holding a piece of paper in his hand.

It was old, so often folded up that it almost fell apart. He gave it to me, and he said, "Please, read it. You have to help me. I am your brother!" I then saw that the paper he held out to me was his baptismal certificate.

Two parishes in Washington, D.C., an Episcopal one and a Catholic one, decided to celebrate Pentecost together one year. Both parishes served a variety of ethnic groups: white and Afro-American English-speaking parishioners; Central American and Latin American Spanish-speaking parishioners; French-speaking Haitians; Portuguese-speaking Brazilians; and Vietnamese-speaking parishioners. They all had their own hymn books, their own symbols, their own music, and their own prayers. Meetings were organized to arrange for the celebration. The interdenominational hurdles were ecumenically overcome without too much difficulty. The cultural arrangements (what languages? which hymns? what kind of decorations?) were more complicated, but they also were finally arranged. After the liturgical services (identical worship solemnities in both church buildings) a big potluck dinner with traditional food, drinks, music, dancing, and singing would close the celebration. The program promised to be a real treat from all points of view.

In one of the last meetings the group became aware of one final hurdle. Some of the richer people in the parishes employed the poorer ones. The social relationship between those two groups was far from ideal. The workers were underpaid because they were illegal immigrants. Their working conditions were substandard. It would be difficult to sit at the same table after the liturgical ceremony and pick up the unjust working relationships on Monday. In fact, they decided, it would be impossible. The celebration did not take place. The time was not yet ripe to extend what was possible in the church buildings to the everyday life of the market square and the labor market. The organizing committee regretfully decided to postpone the festival and to work at making it—politically and socially—possible in the future.

AN ACTIVITY WITH POLITICAL MEANING

Proclaiming from Jesus' Spirit in us that all humanity forms one body is at the same time a statement on how our world should be organized. It is a social, economic, and even political statement. When the eucharist is celebrated in a spiritually awake community, the experience will by itself lead to a felt need to extend the sharing around the altar to concrete actions of justice in society.

Being baptized and baptizing in the name of a God who is the Parent to all of humanity and creation, in whose Word we are all created, and whose Spirit contains the life of the whole of the human family and creation, is an activity with political meaning. Any church from which actions of justice and peace-making do not begin to flow is betraying the Spirit of the God it prays to. Such a community is not faithful to the Spirit that brought it together. It is here that the dialogue with others, and with fellow human beings who are nonbelievers, gets a new, practical dimension. In practically all cases it is quite a struggle to realize in our world our new sensitivity to the absolute value of each individual human person. This value does not depend on baptism, but for the Christian believer finds its formalization and its sacramental expression in that sacrament of initiation. All those who accept with us the *Universal Declaration of Human Rights* are our partners in this struggle. We find our motives in the religious inspiration of the gospel touching our inner spirit; others find it in their own beliefs and convictions, thanks to the divine Spirit — consciously or subconsciously — present in them.

This does not mean that we will know how to vote in an election. How to realize politically the justice and the equality we want to obtain is not something we can read directly from Jesus' life. We know better *what* we want, and even better what we *don't* want in these issues of human rights, than we know *how* to realize and obtain it. No political party seems to have the human/divine covenantal project of the kingdom of God as its program. That is why no church should identify itself with any of those parties. We should, however, be in favor of the policy that comes nearest to the ideal, helping it at the same time to get nearer! In other words, we should be politically engaged. The organization of justice and peace belongs to our mission task. How to do it provokes much discussion.

THE EARLY COMMUNITIES

The first Christian communities faced the same problems. They went to the Temple, had their eucharistic get-togethers afterward, and in no time decided that they had to do something about their social and economic relationships. They organized an inter-ethnic food distribution system and began a new economic set-up among themselves. Luke tells the story in the Acts of the Apostles. He describes different ways in which communities took care that "there were no needy persons among them" (Acts 4:34). In one case they kept their own property, but shared with those in need (Acts 4:32). In another case they sold what they had, brought the proceeds to the apostles, who then distributed it according to the different needs (Acts 4:34-35). There were even more fundamental justice issues at stake. Paul and Peter discussed vehemently whether non-Jews had to become Jews before being admitted to the new communities. This is an issue that arises in new ways again and again in our own communities: Must the "others" become like us before we accept them? This question will be discussed in the next chapter.

UNCOMFORTABLE IMPLICATIONS

The praying of the Our Father, the singing of Mary's Magnificat, the reciting of the prophets, the reading of the gospels, Paul's letters about our oneness in Christ and the forgiving of the human past, and the book of Revelation all have political implications. No wonder that discussion is often fierce—and sometimes leads to the rejection of God's plans for the human family. Too many of us get upset when we hear about Christian projects for the transformation of society. Our discomfort betrays us. We know, from deep down within, what would happen if we relate our worship to the ideals of justice, empowerment, liberation, conscientiza-tion, education, and the fostering of human equality. Some of us are—consciously or subconsciously—afraid that we would have to live with implications we are not eager to confront. The more we profit from the actual corrupt and sinful situation in the world, the more afraid we might be. Yet, as Belgian theologian Edward Schillebeeckx wrote:

> The nature and the duty of the Christian faith and thus also the official church is to further truth and justice in the world in the way of a spiritual power, critical and ethical, a power which has as its mission keeping alive in the heart of humanity the will to form human soci-ety in a *polis*, a city, a dwelling-place in which it is good for everyone to live, something which it is good to live for.[1]

This goodness is recognizable; it was revealed in Abram and Sarai as present as the ideal and dream in the human heart. It is God's own project, which reaches from within us together in this world out to beyond this world for all time to come. This vision, as presence, broke through in its full-ness in the person of Jesus.

LIFE IN THE SPIRIT

When the good news about Jesus activates a human community for the first time, the reaction is at its freshest. It was so in Jerusalem; it is the case nowadays. A newly baptized adult is almost always more fervent than those who have been baptized for years and years. When the vibrations of Jesus touch a human community for the first time, great things happen. In the older Christian communities the Spirit too often has been interpreted, canonically regulated, and in a sense almost domesticated. It is in the young churches that the Spirit's work is most visible.

I remember a meeting of forty lay workers and some priests in the last week of June 1983 at Kanamai Conference Center near Mombassa in Kenya. They represented the Christian Development Education Service. During the meeting the diocesan development education programmers reported on their activities in the small Christian parish communities. The list of those church development projects was long and revealing. It was not so much a list of retreats or Bible study classes or pastoral seminars or prayer groups. It was a list that ran from water projects to the building of one-room houses for the disabled, from intensive agriculture projects to literacy programs, from management and leadership courses for women to demonstrations on the use of semi-arid land, from tree planting to teaching better cooking methods. And all this was done inter-ethnically! Almost all of them complained that many priests, in some regions more than 75 percent, had difficulties working with the groups, because they did not think the projects "spiritual" enough. But the communities were all sure that it was what the Spirit moved them to do. I remember how one of them burst out: "But it is what they did in the Acts of the Apostles in Jerusalem!"[2]

We should not, however, make light of the work of the Holy Spirit in older communities. The Spirit continually inspires those who are willing to listen; a praying community cannot escape the Spirit's impulses. A good example in the United States, similar to the one just mentioned in Kenya, is the Campaign for Human Development, the official development program of the United States Catholic Conference.[3] It helps bridge economic, social, and ethnic differences through a well-tested program that helps different groups — sometimes in the same parish, sometimes in the same locality or region — to help in one another's growth and development.

Thousands of justice and peace networks cover the United States from parish to parish, often networking with the rest of the world. They empower refugees and battered women, abused children and dumped senior citizens, and those who write themselves off as valuable members of society because they have been written off by others. They organize "bread and fish" for the homeless and poor. They help to twin inner-city parishes with those more affluent.

Some join Amnesty International as a Christian community and open their doors to all kinds of people who come together to support each other in the rebuilding of their self-esteem and freedom. Others join the Advent Tree of Compassion, the September Hunger Month Observance, and the October Respect for Life Celebration. They visit the sick and give free legal advice for those who need it. They organize convocations and retreats on the social message in the Bible. They mediate in conflicts to avoid the hassle, the antagonism, and the cost of legal procedures. They monitor the legislative processes of advocacy for the poor and powerless in their states and national assemblies with their sophisticated electronic networks and bulletin boards. Participants in some of those networks, like the Sanctuary movement, no longer define themselves as nationals of one country, but as citizens of the kingdom of God. They try to exercise greater control over the evils in their society by using tools such as "Social Analysis,"[4] developed by the Center of Concern. They are in contact with Christians and others struggling for justice, peace, and environmental integrity in all parts of the world.

AT THE CENTER OF LIFE

The Spirit of God is alive and well in millions of ways, although its fire has to be kindled in many more human beings and the communities they form. It has to be aroused not only in activities and responses such as the ones we just mentioned, but in the very center of our life. Gathering the nations, healing and empowering, realizing justice and making peace were not extras in the lives of Jesus and Mary. Mary did not become the mother of God in her free time or as a volunteer. It was her life. Our mission and task are not an extra either, as religion and piety often are for those who only think of them on Sunday or at Christmas or Easter. Our mission and task are not for "amateurs." They should fill our personal, family, and community life; they should be the heart of our educational and professional activities.

SEEKING THE VISION

The vision seen by Abram and Sarai—and put into words in so many stories and parables, sounds and tongues in the Jewish and Christian Scriptures—does not speak only of a "saved" and "liberated" human family where all will be brothers and sisters, all friends; where no master-servant relationships will exist; where pain and tears will be wiped away and forgotten. The vision imaged also a lasting city, where God will be with us forever and ever; where all nations and individuals will share their national and personal splendor to the joy of all. They even saw in that New Jerusalem a bright sky, crystal clear living water, and fruit and green leaf-bearing healing trees. They saw, like John did in his visions later, an undamaged "new heaven and new earth" (Rv 21:1). This vision is of the heaven and the earth we all carry as our destiny in the deepest of our beings. It is this vision we realize at the peak points of our lives — in love-making, in shared beauty and joy, during a festival or dance, in a choir, a concert or successful team work, in prayer and ecstasy. We invoke a oneness with the whole of inorganic and organic nature when we commemorate Jesus' life, death, and resurrection with bread *"given by the earth"* and wine, *"the fruit of the vine,"* forming Jesus Christ's body and blood for and with us.

Every believer, of whatever conviction, faces a world that needs healing. The fact that we know things are not as they should be is another indication of the Spirit we carry in our-selves. We are falling apart; injustice is rampant; the power-ful are exploiting the weak; some have and consume almost all the world's produce while others are starving. Drugs and drink are destroying too many, disease threatens all of us, human services fall short. Ecological disasters are imminent, rivers are polluted, the air is unbreathable, forests disappear, the ozone layer is breaking up, soil erosion and overgrazing destroy the land, the military eats capital that should be used to feed, heal, and educate. The ravages and dangers are so serious that only the deepest motivation can rescue us. That deepest motivation is in us; it is God's Spirit self that makes us reach out to our fulfillment, with God's love in our hearts and full of hope

> not in an indeterminate or undirected way, but in a very definite direction . . . concern for a better society for all men and women, above all for the outcast and marginalized, those who are devastated; pastoral con-cern for communication as an unceasing social and cultural criticism where injustice is evident; concern for the human body, for human psychological and socio-logical health; concern too for the natural human envi-ronment; concern for the wholeness of Christian faith, hope and love; concern for meaningful prayer and for

a meaningful sacrament; and finally concern for the individual pastorate, above all towards the lonely, and those who "no longer hope." Christian spirituality derives both its power and its joy from this eschatological hope in which Christians do all this.[5]

Interreligious dialogue is necessary for all the reasons we mentioned in the preceding chapter. Interreligious action is necessary if we want to save our world and humanity. The World Council of Churches and the Catholic Church formed a joint working group to grapple with these issues in 1965, a cooperation that should be extended to all other religions. A first sign of such a collaboration was realized in Assisi in 1987, when Pope John Paul II invited practically the whole religious world to come together to pray for peace and wholeness.

What cannot be realized as yet at a world scale is often possible at a local level. We need action in solidarity to overcome the dangers that threaten the human family and its environment. All of us should be able to feel at home on this planet.

For Reflection

1. "What does the Lord require of you? Act justly and walk steadfastly" (Mic 6:8). Meditate on this old prophetic saying, thinking of the justice and peace issues in your life. Share your story.

2. Is there a relation between your baptism, the eucharist, and being involved in local and national politics? Discuss.

3. How do you react to the following statement from Walter J. Burghardt, S.J.:

The distance between the rich and the poor continues to widen. One out of every five children in our country is growing up below the poverty line — one out of every three black children. Yet, I still hear devout Catholics insisting that the poor are lazy, that anyone who wants to work can find it, that the single parent with small children should eschew the welfare check and get into the job market with the rest of us. Thirty-seven million Americans have no access to health care; untold thousands of the homeless cram our shelters or huddle over street grates; the elderly rummage through garbage cans for the food we cast away so lightly. Yet, I still hear Catholics complaining that their hard-earned money is being rerouted to wastrels, to those who have no future, who are a drain on the rest of us.[6]

4. Discuss Paul VI's statement:

   Evangelization would not be complete if it did not take into account the unceasing interplay of the Gospel and of man/woman's concrete life, both personal and social.[7]

5. After having worked for years in an impoverished inner-city community, a lay leader in the parish had to leave. At his farewell he was thanked by the community for having given them hope. Comment.

CHAPTER 16

About Feeling at Home: Inculturation

My Father will love him and we will come to him and make our home with him.

(John 14:23)

I nculturation is a new word. The most complete English dictionary, the Oxford English Dictionary, does not even mention it in its latest (1991) edition. Yet many theologians use the word. Pope John Paul II has used it several times to express the need to help people welcome Jesus in their own culture and to make them feel "at home" in the church.

REFRESHING AN OLD CONCEPT

The word inculturation might be new, but the idea and the practice are not. When Paul announced the good news in Athens, he began by looking around the city to get some information about its inhabitants. He must have visited a library, because he quotes two of the local poets. The quotation he used from the Greek poet Epimenides, "For in him we live and move and have our being," the church still uses in one of its Sunday preface prayers celebrating the eucharist. Paul was not very successful, but he tried to make his audience feel "at home" in what he was telling them. So the idea and the practice are far from new, but they have been so overlooked that to refresh this approach we needed to coin that new word, *inculturation*.

In the pluralistic world in which we live, travel, and work, most of us know from experience that our home culture is different from the culture of many of the people we meet. When I invited Africans to my table in East Africa, the table was laid in the Western way, a knife, a fork, and a spoon next to each plate. My visitors would use that cutlery without comment. But, when I invited them to make themselves at home, they wouldn't use the cutlery. Before we began to eat, they would ask where they could wash their hands. They would wash them, dry them carefully, and return to table to eat with their hands. Once I asked them for the reason. At first they were a bit embarrassed to tell me. Finally they explained that eating with the hands is more hygienic than eating with "those iron tools." Who was the last one to eat from them? Had they been well washed? Who had washed them? They could be absolutely sure of the cleanliness of their own hands. While I, with my Western mentality, thought that eating with a fork and a knife was more hygienic than eating with my hands, they thought the opposite. So I learned why in East African restaurants the first thing the waiters and waitresses do is to present a big bowl, some soap powder, and a jug of water to let the customers wash their hands.

CULTURE SHOCK

Being polite in one culture can be impolite, even shocking, in another culture. Asking "How is your wife?" is polite in Anglo-Saxon circles; it is offensive in other contexts. Tilt-

ing your plate the wrong way when finishing the last spoon-
ful of soup can be highly offensive. The same word might
have different meanings, even when you speak about Jesus.
Africans who hear that Jesus came to bring us "life to the
full," often call him, as a consequence, their "ancestor" —
something unlikely to occur to a Western Christian. African
traditional marriages are in general organized in a way different from those Westerners are familiar with. For them, it
is a matter between two families, not so much a contract
between two individuals. Child bearing also plays a different
role than it does in the West.

All these differences cause difficulties when cultures
meet. Christian communities have had such problems from
the very beginning. Peter and Paul debated whether non-
Jewish Christians had to be circumcised, because they
themselves as Jews had been circumcised. They discussed
what kind of meat people were allowed to eat, how it had to
be slaughtered, and with whom they were allowed to sit at
table. Often the issues themselves had hardly any real
importance, but these details helped people feel at home —
or not.

MOVING TOWARD THE NEW JERUSALEM

In the final outcome, in the New Jerusalem, everyone will
feel at home. Organizing and preparing the kingdom of God
in this world has to take that desire into account. For years
we used unleavened hosts that were baked in Holland and
wine grown and bottled in France during the eucharist in
the heart of Africa. It was sometimes difficult to convince
Africans that those hosts were real food. It was difficult to
explain to them why the wine, which they had no difficulty
in recognizing as drink, had to come in those fancy bottles
or barrels from Europe. When Jesus celebrated with his
friends at the last supper he did so in a context they knew,

with food they ate, and drink they were accustomed to. It
was a typical Middle East Jewish meal; bread and grape
wine are Middle East cultural elements. But when we celebrate the same meal in his memory somewhere in the African Highlands, or in an American or European city, the
food used is foreign to us. Not only Africans, but Westerners too have to explain to our children that the host is
bread.

The food we eat and the wine we drink during those
meals are not the only differences. In some African cultures
it is customary for women and men to eat separately.The
men eat together; the women eat together with the children.
Sometimes it is the custom to eat in silence. Celebrating
the eucharist is done by men, women, and children
together, and many words are spoken and hymns sung.
Many African Christians would love to use their own food to
express their unity with Jesus and through him with each
other. Many are happy that the inequality that culturally
existed between women and men begins to be overcome in
their celebration of the eucharist, through being together
with their common oldest family member and age-mate
Jesus Christ in the home of God. Vincent Donovan reports
that,

> Masai men had never eaten in the presence of women.
> In their minds, the status and condition of women
> were such that the very presence of women at the time
> of eating was enough to pollute the food that was
> present. How then was Eucharist possible? In their
> minds it was not. If ever there was a need for Eucharist
> as salvific sign of unity, it was here. I reminded them
> that besides the law of love which I had preached to
> them and they had accepted, I had never tried to inter-
> pret for them how they must work out that law in their
> homes and in their lives, and in their treatment of their
> daughters and wives and female neighbors. . . . But

here, in the Eucharist we are at the heart of the
unchanging gospel that I was passing on to them.
They were free to accept that gospel or reject it, but if
they accepted it, they were accepting the truth that in
the Eucharist, which is to say "in Christ, there is neither slave nor free, neither Jew nor Greek, neither
male nor female." They did accept it, but it was surely
a traumatic moment for them, as individuals and as a
people, that first time when I blessed the cup, or
gourd in this case, and passed it on to the woman sitting next to me, told her to drink from it, and then
pass it on to the man sitting next to her. I don't
remember any pastoral moment in which the "sign of
unity" was so real for me. And I was not surprised
some time later when a group of teenage girls told me
privately, that the *"ilomon sidai"* (good news), that I
talked about so constantly, was really good news for
them.[1]

This example shows that being invited to the house of
God, the conscious or subconscious ultimate hope and
desire of every human being, is not only something cross-
cultural using African cultural elements, but it is also something that corrects and amends a culture. It brings people
together in the name of Jesus in a way they were never
together before. Didn't we say that Jesus came to gather
and heal the scattered children of God?
    The same Masai in their turn corrected Father Donovan
from within their cultural setup on this same point of
togetherness. When he had come to the end of his evangelization and was going to give the final preparation for baptism, he told the group of neophytes that he congratulated
them. Then he added that one of them, an old man who
had been herding his cattle too often during instruction
time, and an old woman, who according to him scarcely
believed, could not be baptized. At that point an old man,
Ndangoya, interrupted him:

"Padri, why are you trying to break us up and separate us? During this whole year that you have been teaching us, we have talked about these things when you were not there, at night around the fire. Yes, there have been lazy ones in our community, but they have been helped by those who are intelligent. Yes, there are the ones with little faith in this village, but they have been helped by those with much faith. Would you turn out and drive off the lazy ones and the ones with little faith and the stupid ones? From the first day I have spoken for these people. And I speak for them now. Now, on this day a year later, I can declare for them and for all this community, that we have reached the step in our lives where we can say: *'We believe.'* "[2]

Donovan adds: *"We believe.* Communal faith. Until that day I had never heard of such a concept." And then he wonders whether he did hear of it but had overlooked it completely. Don't we ask questions at the baptism of a baby that cannot be answered by the child, but are answered by its community? The Masai definitely clarified something for Donovan that day.

Father Donovan clarified things for them as well. He told the story of Jesus under a full moon in Great Rift Valley. An old warrior stood up and said, "I know what you are telling us, that those others—and he pointed to the other side of the hills in the distance, where their traditional enemies lived—belong together with us to the same family." Some accepted this new challenge; others did not. They all understood that it would mean a whole change of life.

JESUS' SONG OF UNITY

Scholars at the Department of Philosophy and Religious Studies in Nairobi, Kenya, did some research on the psy-

chology of conversion, as they called it. The gospel story
that influenced most "converts" to make their step was the
one of the Good Samaritan. The story recounts how a man
from one ethnic group, a Samaritan, opened his heart and
his purse to a victim who belonged to another ethnic group,
a Jew. When they heard that story, when Jesus sang that
song to them, his listeners started to burn from within. They
discovered in themselves what they always had hoped for:
to be loved together by God and to be invited to God's
home. When they heard Jesus sing his song, they heard it
coming from within themselves! That melody is indeed in all
of us! Pope Paul VI said it well to Africans in Kampala,
Uganda:

> It will require an incubation of the Christian "mystery"
> in the genius of your people in order that its native
> voice more clearly and frankly may then be raised har-
> moniously in the chorus of the other voices in the uni-
> versal church.[3]

We have to organize ourselves in such a way that newcomers feel at home with us; they have to take care that we
find ourselves at home with them. We have to sing the
Jesus song hidden in our hearts and minds together! It is
the same kind of interplay we found in our dialogue and our
work at justice, peace, and a clean environment. We have to
be faithful to ourselves and to them. They have to be faithful
to themselves and to us. It seems a difficult, almost impossible task. John Paul II warns that it will be a slow process,
but it is a process that is called for by the divine impulse in
us, homing in on Jesus organizing with us the "great camp
meeting in the Promised Land."

THE ATTRACTION OF JESUS

When this process is well entered in a good dialogue,
everyone feels at ease and at home. If we discover in the

words of the other our deepest self, how could those words
be strange to us? Bernard Bassett, S.J., once marveled that
so many people were and are attracted by Jesus. It was not
his money, because he had none. It was not his background, which was the simplest possible. His appearance
was probably very ordinary. It was not his academic learning; he simply did not have it. He was not a politician. He
made no nationalistic speeches. Was it his miracles? Bassett
notes that at first sight this might be the answer. He then
decides it is not. He explains that at critical moments Jesus
failed to hold a crowd. It was not his learning, not his looks,
not his miracles, but the ease with which others could be
themselves in his company. Nicodemus, Zacchaeus, Levi,
the Roman officer, the adulterous woman, the Samaritan
woman, Martha, Mary, the twelve, and so many others. All
of us can feel at home with him, because he responds to
the "red-hot point of consciousness."[4] His approach assures
us of our personal and everlasting value; loving us in that
way he promises us fullness of life. He makes us feel at
home, because that is what love does. It takes away all fear.
It allows us to be ourselves. We are destined to be at home
with one another, a home where we celebrate each other
and ourselves, bringing together our splendor and gifted-
ness — the home of the vision first glimpsed by Abram and
Sarai.

THE SCOPE OF INCULTURATION

Inculturation is an issue in our contact with people from
far-away countries and neighbors who live in ways foreign to
us. It is also an issue in our own local context. That is
apparent to anyone who studies the faces of people who are
in church for a funeral or marriage. We see people who are
not accustomed to a church building; the uneasy pews; the
raised altar; the clothes worn by the celebrants; the lan-

guage spoken; the symbols used; the stress laid on blood
and sacrifice. Perhaps the impression is given that some
people hardly count, and that others are not only more
important but basically different.

We notice it when we try to explain to teenagers the traditional approach to Jesus suffering for them; when we speak
about a God who got upset about the sinfulness of this
world, condemned it, and was only willing to look at it again
after Jesus would have shed his blood in expiation for us.
Here, too, we face the inculturation issue. Teenagers, and
people of all ages, are often unable to place this kind of
God. The story about Jesus has to be told in a way that
remains faithful to it but also is understandable in modern
culture. His story is a truth that is needed by all, but it
should be communicated in a relevant manner, touching
the "red-hot point" of modern consciousness — a consciousness that is often aware of our need to change, to be
together, to respect human rights, to heal, to make peace,
to respect the environment, and to build a more human
city. This is a consciousness that reaches back to that early
vision of Abraham and Sarah. For the fulfillment of such a
dream, many have been willing to put their lives on the line,
as Jesus did. It is a universal hope for a world of peace and
wholeness, a hope teenagers and seniors alike are well able
to understand.

"AT HOME" IN COMMUNITY

It is very difficult to feel at home in a hotel room. The lay-
out, the decorations, and the furniture — in fact everything —
are imposed on you from above. Whether a person comes
from India, Africa, Europe, or the North Pole, whether he or
she is old or young, all get the same kind of room. Feeling
at home cannot come from above. It can only come from
the grassroots. To make others (and ourselves) feel at home

or inculturated in the church asks for another model of
church than the one we are accustomed to. The new model
was foreseen by the Second Vatican Council, when it
described the church as the People of God before mentioning the ministries needed to keep those communities in
contact with one another.[5] The People of God in their small
communities—in all their variety—are the core and sub-
stance of the church. The good news finds its roots in such
communities, and nowhere else.

These communities form together the body of Christ,
another image (and reality) that indicates how much we
should be able to feel at home, as much at home as in our
own skin. It also means that these communities need ministries and organizational patterns to keep in contact and
communion. That is why there were "over-seers" (*episko-
poi*, or bishops). They are meant to keep the necessary
contacts to foster a process in which the whole of the world
will be knit together, just as a body of a new human being
is formed in the womb of its mother.

This model is not clerical. It has confidence in the capac-
ity of Christian communities themselves to discern the Spirit
and to realize the gospel at the grassroots level. Pope John
Paul II speaks of this reality when he mentions the differences among the four gospels,

> . . . a pluralism which reflects different experiences and
> situations within the first Christian communities. It is
> also the result of the driving force of the Spirit self, it
> encourages us to pay heed to the variety of missionary
> charisms and to the diversity of circumstances and
> peoples. . . . The four gospels therefore bear witness
> to a certain pluralism within the fundamental unity of
> the same mission.[6]

Jesus lived his life and told his story in a way that made
others discover themselves within their own persons and
within their own communities. It also made them discover

how closely they are linked and how organically bound together. It is the story about the branch and the vine: "I am the vine, you are the branches" (Jn 5:5). It is interesting to note how he speaks of us as branches, not as individual leaves, but as bundles of leaves, families of leaves and flowers, branches. That is how the story should be told, and also how it should be lived. We flourish not only in the circle of our own community, our children and grandchildren, but also with all the others around us. If we listen to the Spirit in us asking us to work at justice and peace, at the gathering of the nations and the healing of the world, we will reach out to all those around us. We do so not to impose ourselves, but to exchange our spiritual experiences; to find out how God and God's Spirit is reflected in thousands of ways in all cultures; to express that we all belong together. And then fear may give way to love (cf. 1 Jn 4:18), and we will be on our way to a fulfillment and salvation more varied, colorful, and at the same time more harmonious than we ever expected in our wildest dreams. We sometimes find glimpses of this age-old vision when we are culturally together in prayer, celebration, and feast. It is a good reason to come together in those ways as often as we can!

The Christian community is the community where everyone should feel at home. It is only in such "home" communities that we can find the safety and security we need to feel at ease, to be happy, and to grow to fulfillment. It is only when these communities are interconnected that all of us, gathering together and at peace with one another, can heal, prosper, and strive after our final destiny, can follow the vision of our forebears. Even then a lot of things still have to happen, which leads us to our final chapter on our mission.

For Reflection

1. "To understand the others, we must not annex them, but rather make ourselves their guests" (Louis Massignon). Discuss.

2. "A cat thrown in water will be able to tell more about that water than a fish swimming in it." Do you agree?

3. Read in all four gospels one event in the life of Jesus, for example, his agony in the garden of Gethsemane, or the reasons he gives for his death on the cross. How do they compare?

4. Would your parish community be willing to organize a transcultural festival?

5. Are you reaching out to those who do not belong to your own circle? Do you ever help others think about those who are not here? How can you do so?

CHAPTER 17

How to Organize and Manage Our Mission

For the people in this world are more shrewd in dealing with their own kind than are the people of the light.

(Luke 16:8)

 et us begin with a fairy tale. It is a tale children tell. And it is a story we sometimes tell our children. It is in a way what is told in any fairy tale with a happy ending. This is the story:

Something had happened to the world, or rather, to the human family inhabiting it. Everybody was filled with love, mutual understanding, and good will. Nobody could explain how it had happened. Was it because of the natural disasters that had ravaged the world—floods, volcanoes, earthquakes? Was it because of the human disasters—the violence and race riots that had hit the streets and whole communities? Was it because of all the conventions that had taken place, or because of all the meditations that had put people in touch with themselves and the presence of the divine in them? Was it because many people had been hum-

ming together the same song? Nobody knew. Yet a
change had taken place. Evil was gone, the abusive
foster parents had died, the dragons had been killed,
the fierce giant and the evil witch had changed their
ways, and all were ready to live happily forever and
ever.

HAPPILY EVER AFTER

The stuff of fairy tales indeed. Yet, let us imagine that
tomorrow morning all people in the world come into contact with the light of God in themselves; that they all wake
up full of God's love for themselves, each other, and the
whole of the world. Would that change of heart change the
world? No, it wouldn't. It would only be a beginning. The
world would still have to be changed in its structures.
Justice and peace would still have to be established. We
would have to forgive the past and to become reconciled
with one another. We would need conventions, seminars,
workshops, symposiums, and meetings to work out new
arrangements and networks. We would have to change the
educational and health systems, the use and distribution of
resources, transportation, communication, environmental
policies, agriculture, industry, and the arts. Good will on its
own does not guarantee a political system that does justice.
That system would have to be invented, tested, amended,
and developed. The good will would help in doing it, but the
City of God would still have to be built. The celebration of
being together would still have to be organized.

That good will does not exist. Or better, it does, but it is
still hidden, tucked away in our hearts and minds. How
many of us, people of the Book, who call ourselves Jews,
Christians, or Muslims, are aware and live the dynamism
that made Abram and Sarai leave their old life and seek a
vision they barely glimpsed? How many Christians live the

dynamism that made Mary accept her role, and Jesus live, die, and rise? Our first *mission* task is to discover and advertise that dynamism in ourselves and in one another.

CONVERSION FROM WITHIN

To do so demands a turn-around, a change of heart, a giving-in to God's love in us. It means lending our ears to God, listening "to the cries of the poor." It means conversion, not an easy thing. When Jesus became aware of the Holy Spirit in his life, and when he heard the voice saying, "This is my beloved son" at his baptism by John (Mt 3:17), he went for forty days to the desert, where he was tempted not to give in to God's call. It is the temptation we find in the lives of those who do heroic things for justice or peace, but also in the lives of those who dedicate themselves to less ostentatious kingdom of God issues. All of us are tempted to say, "I know that this is what I must do now, though I would prefer to do something else and take it easy." Jesus did not give in to that temptation, though it was with him all his life. He decided to make God's call the project of the rest of his life.

SEEKING SUPPORT

It is difficult to resist temptation alone. Nobody who ever succeeded in following God's vision and promise did so alone. Too many thresholds have to be passed, too much fear overcome, too many obstacles cleared, too many addictions mastered, too much resistance and confusion overcome. The first thing Mary does after her self-giving yes is to go to Elizabeth. It is when Elizabeth affirms and supports her that she sings out her hope and expectations. The first thing Jesus does on his first walk along the lake side is to look for company, going so far as inviting people he accidentally met. He could take that risk, because he knew that his dream was the stuff their dreams were made of. Looking for company is also the last thing he does before being arrested, asking the same companions not to leave him alone in his anguish. It is together with his friends that he engages himself to the kingdom of God, washing their feet, breaking his bread, sharing his wine, and revealing to them his and their own dynamism and Spirit.

How far have we made this dynamism and Spirit of his our own? We accepted it formally as present in us at our baptism. That was, however, only the beginning. Many of us don't come any further, just as many are quite willing to celebrate Jesus' birth at Christmas without wanting to go all the way with him for the rest of the liturgical year. During the same initiation rite we were also anointed priest, prophet, and king, which determines our whole personal and social existence. How far is that true in the reality of our life? How many of us put ourselves at the service of God's kingdom?

A WEAKNESS TO OVERCOME

I am thinking of a nurse in a large hospital in the United States, well-trained and highly efficient. She does a good job, is kind and pleasant to her patients. Yet she is dissatisfied with her way of life. After praying and attending retreats she comes to the conclusion that she would like to do something directly for the reign of God here on earth.

She contacts a mission organization that is willing to send her out as an associate. She follows the training program and goes overseas to work in a hospital. She remains there for three years, the limit allowed by the organization that sent her. Now she is back in the same hospital from which she left.

The strange thing about her story is that in her mind and that of the church community she belongs to she only seemed to be working for the reign of God while "volunteering." It was only in the context of a religious, clerical position that she was able to integrate her profession into her view of the reign of God. Once back in her original parish community, she feels things are again just as they were before she left.[1]

This story points to a weakness in our Christian approach, a weakness that affects much volunteerism not only in the church but in the society at large. People set aside "volunteer" time as a kind of self-corrective for a situation in which they have—in a way—banned the Spirit of Jesus from their daily professional and personal lives. This promotes a kind of Sunday Christianity decried by a clerical institution that often has caused it by giving the impression that the spiritual domain was its exclusive own.

THE TOTAL VISION

The dynamism of Jesus' Spirit reaches into our hearts and minds, but it is often far from being the heart and soul of our existence. It was not like that for Abraham and Sarah, for Mary and Joseph, for Jesus. They related to each other, to God, and to their community in view of their vision and hope in God's promise. They begot and educated their offspring taking into consideration the realization of that vision. It filled their whole family and professional life. As we noted before, Mary was not Jesus' mother in her spare time. The vision of the kingdom of God must fill the whole of our existence. Its realization is the core of our lives, the reason of our existence. The mission of realizing the vision is ours; it is the mission of the People of God:

It is clear that from the very origins of Christianity, the
laity — as individuals, families and entire communities —
shared in spreading the faith. . . . The need for all the
faithful to share in this responsibility is not merely a
matter of making the apostolate more effective; it is a
right and duty based in their baptismal dignity,
whereby "the faithful participate for their part in the
threefold mission of Christ as priest, prophet and
king." Therefore "they are bound by the general obligation, and they have the right, whether as individuals
or in associations, to strive so that the divine message
of salvation may be known and accepted by all people
throughout the world. This obligation is all the more
insistent in circumstances in which only through them
people are able to hear the gospel and know Christ"
. . . they especially are called "to seek the kingdom of
God by engaging in temporal affairs and ordering
these in accordance with the will of God."[2]

It is our task to realize humanity's deepest aspirations put
in us by God our creator and lover. We are called by God's
Spirit in us to realize the kingdom of God. That is our task,
whatever our sex, age, marriage status, profession, or skill.
It is not a question of volunteering as a doctor in a clinic for
homeless people for some hours during the weekend; or as
a lawyer spending some hours giving free legal advice to
people who would not be able to pay for it; or as a parish-
ioner cutting the grass around the church building without
asking for payment. It is in our work and our family life that
God's Spirit should be our heart and our soul. The way wife
and husband love each other and relate to their children;
the way children relate to their parents and to their future;
the way professionals and workers render their professional
services and are politically engaged; the way the pope, bishops, priests, and deacons organize their pastoral and sacramental ministry, all relates to this mission and task in the

world. Healing, nursing, producing food, transporting, trading, educating, doing research, banking, investing, managing, servicing, organizing, associating, preaching, and worshiping, all should be seen in the light of that most divine of human visions: the final destination of the whole of the human/divine family. It is because of our universal engagement in this task that we should be attracting others by witnessing to our vision in our approach to life. We should open the dialogue with them in view of our common goals of a just and peaceful world.

HEALING AND GATHERING IN COMMUNITY

All over the world Christian communities are beginning to reorganize themselves into communities with educational, medical, self-help, and development projects, beneficial to themselves and to the wider world. The older male and female religious congregations and societies — which often started as lay movements but almost always got clericalized! — are beginning to share their charisms, residences, and tasks with lay people, families, and sometimes whole Christian communities. Outsiders join communities of contemplative congregations while continuing to live their professional lives as doctors, lawyers, car mechanics, or waitresses.

New associations and societies group professionals together to make it possible for them to organize their lives and their professionalism more integrally in a kingdom of God context. Some family groups organize their worship, family, and leisure time together. Sometimes they only pray jointly and share their faith experiences. In other cases they bring the money they earn together to make it possible for all of them to be available for professional services to all those in need, rich and poor, at the same time.

Entire parishes are reorganizing themselves to reappro-

priate the healing and gathering tasks they never should
have lost. Parish communities are twinning with Christian
communities elsewhere. The rich befriend the poor; the
poor befriend the rich. In parishes all over the world new
groups are forming that come together for tasks set in view
of renewal, prayer, justice, peace, racial harmony, environmental wholeness, and a better and more loving society. In
Latin and Central America those groups are called Basic
Christian Communities, in Africa Small Christian Communities, in North America and Canada they have all kinds of
names.

Theologian Gregory Baum has spoken about "the explo-
sion of spirituality . . . a new experience of God . . . a
renewal of fidelity to the gospel . . . a development that has
great spiritual authority in the churches."[3] Such development has not escaped the attention of Pope John Paul II:

> These are groups of Christians who, at the level of the
> family, or in a similarly restricted setting, come
> together for prayer, Scripture reading, Catechesis and
> discussion on human and ecclesial problems with a
> view to a common commitment. These communities
> are a sign of vitality within the church, an instrument
> of formation and Evangelization and a solid starting
> point for a new society based on a "civilization of
> love."[4]

A NEW SENSE OF MISSION

The revisioning and redivision of our task seems gigantic.
It is, but the work of reorganization has started. Mission is
no longer seen as relevant only to a group of religious male
and female missionaries. Still, people especially trained and
kept free by communities to contact "others" are needed.
These contacts should not only be made "overseas," a term

that refers to a time that is past. "Others" are in new ways present to us not only far away, but also around the corner of the street in our own residential areas, towns, and cities. All over the world, people have been emigrating, immigrating, and migrating. We are getting more and more mixed in one gigantic network. Electronic connections offer new possibilities for communication. Racial division and ethnic violence, definitely reported more frequently than ever before, are experienced by all as scandalous disasters. The tragedy of division and failure, of neglect and marginalization, are ever more keenly felt.

> Television and junk mail pieces make the global village all too apparent. If you give to one international charity (e.g. Bread for the World), soon you will get mailings reminding you of: world hunger (a near billion malnourished in the world); refugees (millions displaced in El Salvador, Afghanistan, Ethiopia, Sudan, occupied Israel, now also in Jordan and Saudi Arabia); prisons (we build more, rehabilitate fewer inmates and prisoners are, perhaps, those most without voice); the reality of AIDS (growing world-wide and in our country); substance abuse issues in the developed and developing world; prisoners of conscience (Amnesty International deals with 5,000 world-wide); solidarity movements with El Salvador, Guatemala, Haiti, the labor movement; the peace movement, never dead, takes on new life today. Again only those deaf to the news and documentaries, will be unaware of consumerism, world debt, the arms trade world-wide, the corruption of drug and drug trafficking, not only here but in Colombia, Bolivia, and Thailand.[5]

Problems and issues hang together. Concentrating on one brings out all the others. Sickness and consumerism, AIDS and drugs, poverty and sexual abuse, homelessness and the national debt—it is all interrelated. The astronauts saw it looking at our planet from space: we form one organic unit. The whole of humanity is slowly waking up to this interconnectedness. It is humanity's response to God's vision and God's dream, hidden as our vision and our dream in all of us.

In the church we can embrace the whole world and at the same time contact each local community by thinking globally and acting locally. Willing to live God's love for the human family and the whole of creation, we in the church are capable of gathering the scattered children of God. We as Christians cannot do this on our own. We only can do it in dialogue and cooperation with all the others.

Being capable of doing something does not mean actually doing it. It is in the tension between these two that our mission asks for local initiatives and contacts among local communities. The church should be, and to a certain extent already is, a living network that connects individuals, families, and communities in a way different from anything else in the world. Its way, the way of love, is the only way to solve the problems of a world becoming more and more aware of its sinful shortcomings and managerial problems. It is the way to fulfill the dream and the vision of God, hiding as the treasure and the pearl in the hearts and minds of all of us, the dream of being together as one family in the house of God. Living that dream in the reality of his life and waking others up to join in its fulfillment brought Jesus Christ among us. It made Abram and Sarai leave Ur and Haran, the prophets sing, and Mary and Elizabeth joyfully welcome their children.

For Reflection

1. Discuss how marriage and children relate to our mission. Is it understandable that some would choose not to marry in view of our mission? Discuss.

2. The Canadian Episcopal Conference suggested the following work plan to its Christian communities. Do you think you would be able to apply it to your context?

   Our pastoral methodology involves a number of steps: a) to be present and listen to the experiences of the poor, the marginalized, the oppressed in our society; b) to develop a critical analysis of the economic, political and social structures which cause human suffering; c) to make judgments in the light of the Gospel principles concerning social values and priorities; d) to stimulate creative thought and action regarding alternative models for social and economic development; and e) to act in solidarity with popular groups in their struggle to transform society.[6]

3. Is there any effort in your parish to keep the lines of communication open with the rest of the Christian world?

4. Do you have anyone in your parish working as a missionary? How do you relate to that person when he or she returns for leave?

5. Is your liturgy organized in a way "that does justice"? Who is present and who is absent in terms of class, race, lifestyle? Who are in the processions? What about the handicapped—are they ever invited to be lectors, ushers, eucharistic ministers? Is the language sexist? Do the general intercessions broaden the vision of the local community, making all conscious of God's children?[7]

CHAPTER 18

Victory and Celebration

And God will wipe away every tear from their eyes.

(Revelation 7:17)

N ow it is time to sum up. Jesus did this at the end of his life. He did it in different ways. Just before starting the last chapter of his earthly life he took the last piece of bread from the table, broke it, and passed it around with the last of the wine. While doing this he said to them, "This is my body, this is my blood." Eating that bread and drinking that wine they formed his body.

He summed it all up in another way at his ascension. He told his disciples that the Almighty, who had empowered him, had done the same to them. They would do what he did — gathering, overcoming the terrors of the past, healing, and peace-making. He added that they would gradually understand their mission better, and that they would be able to do greater things even than he had done. He assured them that he would be with them always.

The Second Vatican Council brought out this truth as it had never been brought out before, except in the practice of the very beginning of the church. All of us share from within ourselves God's love and God's urge to gather the whole of humanity and the whole of creation. Being taken up in the divine process is not reserved to some or to a special group. It is present in the whole of humankind. Those baptized accept it formally as the reason of our existence. We agree formally to have the nerve, the spirit, and the very feelings of Jesus. We are all taken up in the process that found its fulfillment in him. The mission others more or less reserved for themselves, and which we often gladly left to them, is ours. Being a follower of Jesus means more than living a good personal life and joining in a weekend worship; it determines our whole individual, family, social, and professional life. Some of us will be trained to reach out to those far from us. Those professional and specialized missionaries are needed and should be helped. But they cannot replace our own mission of gathering, reconciling, establishing justice, and making peace. It is a daunting task indeed, but at the same time a meaningful and hope-giving one. It is the *only* meaningful and hope-giving program and spirituality for our day and age.

THE STRENGTH OF THE VISION

We all know of people who are so convinced of one or another mission that they have no time for anything else. Jesus was not like that. He goes to a wedding party and provides wine. He takes his rest periods, his weekends, and holidays. He enjoys a good meal in the house of his friends Martha, Mary, and Lazarus. He had to be serious about his mission, and he is. He even put his life on the line, something most of us are not asked to do.

How did Jesus find such perfect balance for his life? He could live fully because he was sure of the victory and of the final outcome. He encompassed the history of the vision.

When Mary met Elizabeth, she not only sang, she must have danced. She sang a song like the far echo of the song

we finally will sing together when we sing and dance within
the city of God and the heart of the Trinity forever and ever.

The fulfillment of the vision breaks through in every
expression of human love. The love of and for our friends,
brides and grooms, our children, our parents, our community, and even those far away are the first signals of what in
the final instance will be, when God is all in all, and we
together in God. Our last dance will not be an end but the
beginning of something lasting forever and ever, a dance in
which the music, the dance, the folklore festivals, the street
feasts, even our better parties, picnics, holidays, outings,
fairs, and ceremonies only vibrate in the slightest resonance.
They are only an echo of things to come, a surface ripple of
what is already going on deep within and at the center.

In the book of Revelation the difficulties that face us are
described in apocalyptic detail. We fight with dragons and
monsters, worse than in any fairy tale or in our wildest
nightmares. John could write in that way because the issue
is in no doubt. Children don't mind the stench, the awful
colors, the sliminess, the teeth, the claws, the smoke out of
the nostrils, and all kinds of other horrible things in tales of
monsters, as long as they are sure that those monstrosities
are going to be killed or tamed in the end. There is more to
the description in the book of Revelation than this kind of
fictitious horror, but there too the battle is won.

> The Book of Revelation may be gory, surrealistic,
> unnerving, even terrifying. But it contains not a single
> note of despair. Those still in the clutches of the
> Dragon may not yet experience it, but the decisive bat-
> tle has already been won. The early church celebrated
> victory in the midst of calamity. The struggle contin-
> ues, but the issue is no longer in doubt. The far-off
> strains of a victory song already reaches our ears, and
> we are invited to join the chorus. This is the rock on
> which we stand: the absolute certainty of the triumph
> of God in the world.

That is why the celebration of the divine victory does not take place at the end of the Book of Revelation, after the struggle is over. Rather it breaks out all along the way (Rev 1:4-8, 17-18; 4:8-11; 5:5, 9-14; 7:117; 8:1-5; 11:15-19; 12:7-12; 14:1-8, 13; 15:2-4; 16:5-7; 19:1-9).[1]

GOD WILL DANCE

This final victory breaks through not only at the moment of our celebrations, though it does then. It is with us not only when we break his bread and share his wine, though it really is there. The reign of God shines through every time people live and die for the sake of human dignity and a just and peaceful world. We all know stories about these break-throughs, about victims who not only affirmed their own human dignity but also that of those who victimized them.

The end will be — as the Prophet Zephaniah wrote — that God will dance.

The Lord your God is with you. He will take great delight in you, he will quiet you with his love, he will rejoice over you with dancing and singing (Zeph 3:17).

We are still out of step, but the dancing has begun. It is what the three in the Blessed Trinity have been doing from all eternity. We are invited in to their circle. They could have forced their dancing step on us, but instead they invited us. They sent Jesus to us to be our Lord of the dance.

He dances in front of us,
he dances before us,
he dances around us
in the improvised tent
we call church

where we have to get in step,
with him,
but also with all our sisters and brothers
together with the whole of creation,
> one step to the right,
> one step to the left,
> one step forward,
> one step backward,
looking up at the tent lines,
and to the sky
through a hole in the roof,
down to the earth,
out of the tent opening
to the far off sky of a new city.
> Tables are set up,
> name tags distributed,
> committees formed,
> bread is broken,
> wine is shared,
> now and then there is a hush
> as if all are in prayer,
> and then the rehearsals veer off again
> > one step to the right,
> > one step to the left,
> > one step forward,
> > one step backward,
groups are formed,
circles opened,
blessings shared,
oil and water
splashed around
anointings and baptisms,
> a trumpet blast,
> the sound of instruments tuned,
> directives are given,
> maps laid out,

and marked are the roads
leading to our destiny
the home of God self.
Remaining ourselves,
but more and more together
in ever growing ecstasy,
    we are taken up in the swirling movement,
    of the dance
    that is already moving around and ahead,
        one step to the right,
        one step to the left,
        one step forward,
        one step backward,
we are still trying
to catch His rhythm,
and the words of the song,
He sings and pipes
in our midst.
    Others are joining,
    balancing gifts on the top of their heads,
    playing their drums and trumpets,
    adding to a cacophony,
    that sounds more and more
    like a symphony
    the longer it lasts.
It is almost dawn,
the rucksacks are packed,
the children awake,
ready to dance
into the dawn of a new day,
    and we,
    we are on our way!

For Reflection

1. Discuss how you as a person, as a family member, and
   as a worker can structure a mission spirituality.

2. Which obstacles hinder you? In clay, paints, colors, or words express the power that most holds you back.

3. Do you ever celebrate with others the victory of good over evil in your life?

4. Write (separately or in a group) your own perception of the vision of the final outcome of our mission.

Notes

1. MEETING JESUS OF NAZARETH

1. *Decree on the Church's Missionary Activity (Ad Gentes)*, no. 3. In *The Documents of the Second Vatican Council*, ed. Walter M. Abbott, S.J. (New York: America Press, 1966).

2. AROUSED BY JESUS

1. William Herr, *In Search of Christian Wisdom* (Chicago: Thomas More Press, 1991), adapted.

10. RECONCILING PEACE-MAKER

1. Corrie ten Boom, *The Hiding Place* (Old Tappan, New Jersey: Fleming H. Revell Co., 1981), p. 238.
2. Doris Donnelly, *Putting Forgiveness into Practice* (Allen, Texas: Argus Communications, 1982), p. 3.

11. SIGNS, SYMBOLS, AND REALITY

1. Justin J. Kelly, "Absence into Presence, A Theology of Imagination," Warren Lecture Series in Catholic Studies, University of Tulsa, 1991, p. 3.
2. Samuel Taylor Coleridge, *Animae Poetae, From the Notebooks*, ed. E. H. Coleridge (Boston: Houghton Mifflin, 1989). Quoted in Kelly, p. 15.

12. INITIATION, SPIRIT, AND MISSION

1. Julius Nyerere, quoted in P. Scharper and J. Eagleson, eds., *The Radical Bible* (Maryknoll, New York: Orbis Books, 1972), p. 13.

2. *Decree on the Church's Missionary Activity (Ad Gentes)*, nos. 3, 4. In Abbott.

3. Henri Teissier, Archbishop of Algiers, *La Mission de l'Eglise* (Paris: Editions Desclée, 1985), p. 38.

13. OUR MISSION: CHALLENGES AND PRIORITIES

1. *Gaudium et Spes*, 1. In Abbott.

2. John Paul II, *Redemptoris Missio (On the Permanent Validity of the Church's Missionary Mandate)*, *Origins* (31 January 1991), no. 1.

3. Ibid. no. 13.

14. HOW TO PROCLAIM AND DIALOGUE

1. The order "Go!" as such is not found in the text, though it is implied and found in practically all translations. There are two sections in Matthew's final text. First, the apostles come together at the meeting point indicated by Jesus: "Then the eleven disciples went to Galilee, to the mountain where Jesus had told them to go. When they saw him, they worshiped him; but some doubted." Then, in a second section, Jesus takes the initiative: "Then Jesus came to them and said, 'All authority in heaven and on earth has been given to me.' " The verb that follows is a participle meaning "making disciples." They will do this because Jesus' power and authority are with them. See, for example, D. A. Carson, *The Expositor's Bible Commentary, Matthew* (Grand Rapids, Michigan: Zondervan, 1984), p. 596.

2. John Paul II, *Redemptoris Missio*, no. 45.

3. *Heritage and Hope: Evangelization in the United States*, Pastoral Letter on the Fifth Centenary of the Evangelization in the Americas (Washington, D.C.: United States National Conference of Catholic Bishops, 1990).

4. John Paul II, *Redemptoris Missio*, no. 4: "For each one is included in the mystery of redemption and with each one Christ has united himself forever through this mystery."

5. V. J. Donovan, *Christianity Rediscovered*, 8th ed. (Maryknoll, New York: Orbis Books, 1990).

6. Christian van Nispen, *Journées Romaines* (August 6-September 6, 1991). Cf. G. Evers, *Conferentie in Rome over Jezus Christus in de dialoog met de Islam, Tijdschrift voor Theologie*, vol. 32, no. 1 (1991), pp. 83-84.

7. Pope Paul VI, Inaugural address to the second session of the Second Vatican Council, September 29, 1963. Cf. Z. Thundy, et al., *Religions in Dialogue: East and West Meet* (Lanham, Maryland: University Press of America, 1985), p. 149.

8. Robert Ellsberg, ed., *Gandhi on Christianity* (Maryknoll, New York: Orbis Books, 1991), p. ix.

9. See K. Cragg, *The Christ and the Faiths* (Philadelphia: Westminster Press, 1987).

10. Paul VI, *Evangelii Nuntiandi*, Introduction, 1975.

11. David A. Bos, "Community Ministries: The Wild Card in Ecumenical Relations and Social Ministry," *Journal of Ecumenical Studies* 24, 4 (1988): 592-98.

12. *Guidelines and Suggestions for Implementing the Conciliar Declaration, Nostra Aetate*, no. 4 (Vatican City: Vatican Commission for Religious Relations with the Jews, 1975).

13. Pope John Paul II, quoted in E. J. Fisher, "Interpreting *Nostra Aetate* Through Post Conciliar Teaching," *International Bulletin for Mission Research*, vol. 9, no. 4 (October 1985), p. 162.

14. Jorge Mejia, quoted in Fisher, p. 163.

15. Thundy, et al., p. 149.

15. THE WHY AND HOW OF JUSTICE, PEACE, AND CREATIONAL INTEGRITY

1. Edward Schillebeeckx, *Jesus in Our Western Culture: Mysticism, Ethics, and Politics* (London: SCM, 1987), p. 78.

2. Quoted in J. G. Donders, *Non-Bourgeois Theology: An African Experience of Jesus* (Maryknoll, New York: Orbis Books, 1985), pp. 159-60.

3. Campaign for Human Development, USCC, 3211 4th Street N.E., Washington, D.C. 20017-1194.

4. J. Holland and P. Henriot, *Social Analysis: Linking Faith and Justice* (Maryknoll, New York: Orbis Books, 1988).

5. Schillebeeckx, p. 30.

6. Walter J. Burghardt, S.J., *A Faith That Does Justice: Challenge of the Nineties to the Christian Community*, Warren Lecture Series, no. 18, The University of Tulsa (1991), p. 6.

7. Paul VI, *Evangelii Nuntiandi*, no. 29.

16. ABOUT FEELING AT HOME: INCULTURATION

1. Donovan, p. 121.

2. Ibid. p. 92.

3. Paul VI, address to participants in the Symposium of African Bishops at Kampala, 31 July 1969, 2: *AAS* 61 (1969), p. 577.

4. B. Bassett, S.J., *How to Be Really With It: Guide to the Good Life* (New York: Doubleday Image Book, 1971), p. 141.

5. *Lumen Gentium*, chaps. 2, 3.

6. John Paul II, *Redemptoris Missio*, no. 23.

17. HOW TO ORGANIZE AND MANAGE OUR MISSION

1. See J. G. Donders, *Risen Life: Healing a Broken World* (Maryknoll, New York: Orbis Books, 1990), p. 28.

2. John Paul II, *Redemptoris Missio*, no. 51.

3. Gregory Baum, quoted by J. A. Coleman, "The Priest's Spirituality as a Mirror of the Global and Socially Concerned Church," keynote speech to the Conference of Religious Superiors of Men, 1991, p. 10.

4. John Paul II, *Redemptoris Missio*, no. 71.

5. Coleman, pp. 4-5.

6. Canadian Episcopal Conference, "Ethical Reflections on the Economic Crisis," 1983.

7. See J. Empereur, *The Liturgy That Does Justice* (Collegeville, Minnesota: Liturgical Press, 1990).

18. VICTORY AND CELEBRATION

1. Walter Wink, "Victory Songs and Fish Fries," *Sojourners*, vol. 21, no. 4 (May 1992), pp. 28-29.